Ron

I admire the way you care for your team. I hope this book encourages what you already do and gives you tools that you can pass on to your team.

—David

Stan has finally captured the magic of his madness in this practical book that outlines the simple but powerful ways to influence people. Whether you're a pastor, nonprofit leader, or corporate C-suite executive, Stan and David's IMPROVleadership approach will change the way you lead your teams.

Brad Lomenick, founder of BLINC, author of
H3 Leadership and *The Catalyst Leader*

With a front-row seat to the leadership and coaching expertise of both Stan Endicott and David Miller, I could not be more delighted with this practical and inspirational tool kit capturing their wisdom. If we hope to develop leaders who flourish, we must be intentional. IMPROVleadership is not just some hypothetical formula. These are proven skills that I regularly employ in my own coaching.

Nancy Beach, leadership coach, author, and speaker

IMPROVleadership will take you beyond the basics and help you develop the artful nuances of leadership. Stan Endicott and David Miller take a creative but accessible approach to improve how you connect with, coach, and help people grow. This book will serve you as either a "read on the run" or a deep soak—either way, the insights are great!

Dan Reiland, executive pastor at 12Stone
Church, author of *Confident Leader!*

In a world where *leadership* could mean a thousand different things, Stan and David have written a leadership book that finally delivers us to the ethos of the word and then gives us clear and practical ways to let the word develop inside us.

Carlos Whittaker, author of *Moment Maker* and *Kill the Spider*

Improv Leadership isn't a book about you—it's about your team! The practical and powerful leadership principles David and Stan share in these pages will teach you how to bring out the best in your team and empower them to do their best work.

Elle Campbell, cofounder of Stuff You Can Use

improv leadership

Stan Endicott and David A. Miller

WITH CORY HARTMAN

improv
leadership

HOW TO LEAD WELL IN EVERY MOMENT

ZONDERVAN REFLECTIVE

Improv Leadership
Copyright © 2020 by Stan Endicott and David A. Miller

Requests for information should be addressed to:
Zondervan, *3900 Sparks Dr. SE, Grand Rapids, Michigan 49546*

ISBN 978-0-310-11295-2 (hardcover)
ISBN 978-0-310-11297-6 (audio)
ISBN 978-0-310-11296-9 (ebook)

Published in association with Don Gates of the literary agency The Gates Group. www .the-gates-group.com.

Cover design: Historic Agency
Interior design: Denise Froehlich
Interior images: Historic Agency, © Slingshot Group

Printed in the United States of America

20 21 22 23 24 /LSC/ 10 9 8 7 6 5 4 3 2 1

To all the leaders who are tired
of the status quo and are ready
to create a culture where their
team loves what they do

The purposes of a person's heart are deep waters, but one who has insight draws them out.

Proverbs 20:5

Contents

Foreword

Almost twenty years ago, Stan Endicott, one of the co-authors of the book you are holding, gave me a life-altering piece of advice. He said to me, "Mike, never sit at a desk. If you have a desk, they will expect you to sit at it." Today I look back on that conversation, and I can see how that simple statement has profoundly shaped my life. With that small nugget of wisdom, spoken at that moment, all the pieces came into alignment, setting a new course for my life.

Why was that statement so catalytic, such a nuclear truth for me? I felt seen and heard, and I felt empowered and validated. Stan knew how I was wired, and he wanted to bump me in a direction that would allow me to thrive. He knew me well enough to know I would die at a typical desk job. And he knew I would come alive if I was able to follow my own unique path.

What Stan was doing in that conversation twenty years ago was powerful and life-changing. It's called IMPROVleadership.

Now it's your turn to sit under the tutelage of Stan and his coauthor, David. The two of them have partnered together, taking decades of experience in coaching leaders and purifying it down to the most potent competencies. In the pages of this book, you won't find a precise scientific approach or a step-by-step process. Instead, you'll find wisdom that shapes the flow and posture you take in coaching and leading others. IMPROVleadership is more an art than a science—a creative and kinder process to guiding someone's life. IMPROVleadership is about releasing our need to control others and allowing something beautiful to be born.

When Stan spoke into my life and warned me against having a desk, I knew something new had been released inside me. His words gave birth to a way of life, something I could never have imagined at that time. Stan's words unleashed a calling to live my purpose, impact as many people as possible, and live out an epic adventure. And it all started with a little improv—and whole lotta love.

Mike Foster
PEOPLE OF THE SECOND CHANCE

Acknowledgments

To our families:

I (Stan) am grateful to Connie, Sara, Nate, and Crystal for living these stories with me. My dad and mom gave me a childhood that is beyond wonderful. Dad taught me the real "stuff" that is included in this book.

I (David) could not be more thankful to my incredible family. Ashley, Isaac, Noah, and Penny were guinea pigs as we developed the tools we use in our competencies. I spent many a date night with my wife sharing our Six-Sketch Storyboards around the most impactful moments we've had in our marriage or with our kids. Each of you make me better.

To Slingshot Group:

To our friends and colleagues at Slingshot Group—we pinch ourselves every day that we get to do this with each of you. You embody the principles of IMPROVleadership with every leader you coach and every church and nonprofit you staff.

To Will Mancini:

Will not only is one of the best toolmakers we've ever known but also has become a true friend. The tools Will helped to engineer for IMPROVleadership have helped many leaders to become the leader they wish they had. Thanks, Will!

To people we talk with:

Thank you, everyone, for talking with us. The joy that has been gifted to us by spending hours (more than we can count) in conversations with people we love, people we know, people we work with, and for that matter, strangers, is one of the treasures of our lives.

CHAPTER 1

The Cure for the Common Leader

How to Overcome the Cost of Leadership-as-Usual

I (Stan) moved to Southern California in 1975. I made up for what I didn't have—a job—by using what I brought with me from the Midwest.

I brought my love of Jesus and his love for me. I brought my wife, Connie. I brought musical talent that I had honed with years of practice. (That was a very good thing to bring since I hoped to make it in the music business.) But I also brought something else: the example of my dad, Lyle Endicott. Most of the way I go at life I got from him, and that has made all the difference in the world.

I grew up in a small village in southern Illinois, a patch of earth divided by a railroad track running right through the middle of town. It had no stoplights—only a tiny grocery store, a post office, and my parents' furniture store. There was a little diner near the railroad tracks with two pool tables in the back, and every day after school, I would go there to play. (Sometimes I would even sneak over there during lunch.) I especially loved playing a game for advanced pool players called snooker.

One ordinary day in 1963, my dad said to me, "Son, come here a second. I have something for you." Grinning, he handed me a long, thin box that looked like the box for a BB gun. I opened the box, and to my surprise, I saw a professional pool cue with my name engraved on the side and inlaid with ivory. It was beautiful. I had never seen anything like it. But that was my dad—he always gave me gifts he knew I would love, even though I did not ask for them. He paid keen attention to my interests, even when I was unaware that he was doing so. I still have that pool cue. That gift permanently marked my life.

Dad did not treat me that way only because I was his son. He treated me that way because he saw potential in me as a person. In fact, he treated everyone that way.

My parents owned the furniture store in that small town, but people came through the door for more than furniture. My dad was determined to hold customer service as his highest value, which is why customers walked out with furniture. He cared more about them than the furniture he sold them. And the people who worked for Dad knew how much he valued them too.

Prior to building a great retail furniture business, my dad flew a Hellcat fighter in the Navy during World War II. After the war the young pilots at the local airport considered him to be their Chuck Yeager. At ninety-seven years old, Dad can't fly by himself anymore, but he recently flew with a fellow named Chris, a pilot whom he had taught to fly many years ago.

When Chris was in his early twenties, he longed to fly with

my dad. One day the airport manager called to tell him that Lyle Endicott wanted to take him on a flight. Chris was in Dallas at the time, but that did not hold him back. He drove all night to make it to the airport by nine o'clock the next morning. My dad was keenly interested in Chris, and Chris knew it. Twenty-seven years later, I barely had to finish asking Chris to take my dad flying for his birthday. Chris's yes was automatic.

I did not realize it growing up, but all along, my dad taught me the art and soul of leadership. He made a lasting impression by investing in people, and they felt natural loyalty to him—a loyalty that, in this case, left Chris joyfully volunteering to return the favor by investing back into my dad.

Is that joyful loyalty and mutual investment present in your team? Stop for a moment and think about the member of your team who gives you the most headaches. Maybe they are under-performing. Maybe they don't take initiative. Maybe they don't communicate enough information, or maybe they communicate too much. Maybe they start relational fires wherever they go. Or maybe their commitment is in question—you are not sure they are "all in."

And maybe they know it. Maybe they are even telling you that they know what you think about them, but they don't use words to do it. Maybe when you talk, their body is rigid, their face blank. Maybe they have made themselves hard to get ahold of, and they reply to your texts with an enigmatic "OK."

Now imagine having a new relationship with that person. Imagine that whenever you say, "Can I talk to you for a second?" they lean in as eagerly as I did just before my dad surprised me with the pool cue. Imagine that when you make a big ask, they are raring to say yes, just as Chris the pilot did.

Can you picture that? What you are picturing is the result of good leadership.

Leadership moves people to do something for the greater good—often something they would not naturally do. It might be something difficult or costly, maybe even something they really don't like. But because of good leadership, they do it anyway.

Love—love that your people feel within—is the most powerful force in leadership, hands down, bar none. Love compels people to follow you and to cooperate with each other. *Love* as we know it in the English language has so many meanings. But in the context of being a leader, it means being successful at gaining someone's trust to the point that they want to be a part of what you are doing—they want a "seat at your table."

But before your people can feel that love, *you* have to learn how to love them like never before. This book is about how to lead that way, because we need to learn the kind of leadership that inspires our people more than ever.

The Common Model of Leadership

Before we go further, let us tell you a bit more about ourselves.

Stan is the chief culture officer at Slingshot Group. Our mission at Slingshot is to build remarkable teams. One way we do that is by matching churches and nonprofits that are looking for staff with just the right candidate for the job. With the right match, both the candidate and the organization flourish.

The other way Slingshot Group builds remarkable teams is by coaching ministry leaders in their current jobs. We help them to become more effective in what they do and to remove the roadblocks that prevent them from loving their work. Although

Love—love that your people feel within—is the most powerful force in leadership, hands down, bar none.

Stan launched our coaching division, today it is led by David, our vice president of coaching. David came to Slingshot Group having achieved success in NextGen ministry. At Slingshot, he led a team that has placed over two hundred NextGen leaders across the country as well as another team that has coached three hundred–plus leaders and ministry teams.

As you may imagine, we have a wide breadth of experience with church and nonprofit staffs with whom we have engaged as coaches, as placement specialists, and as ministry leaders ourselves. Along the way, we have repeatedly encountered a common model of leadership, especially among lead and executive pastors. Its common features include stereotypical directors, systematic management, and scarce care. We believe that this model of leadership, common though it is, is self-defeating. Not to mention very, very expensive.

Stereotypical Directors

We are convinced that a person of any personality type can lead well. But the world seems to gravitate toward an image of a leader with certain stock characteristics. Conversely, people who fit that stock image tend to rush to fill the leadership opportunities that come their way.

You know the type. (Maybe you *are* the type.) Decisive. Driven. Determined. Comfortable in command (or *un*comfortable when no one else is adequate or available for command).

We even have psychometric labels for such people. In classical medicine they were known as "choleric." They are a high *D* in DiSC or an *ET* combo in Myers-Briggs or have abundant "Fiery Red" energy in Insights Discovery.

When it comes to pastors, the church has an interesting

relationship with the classic director stereotype. Many smaller and more traditional churches are practically allergic to it, vastly preferring pastors on the opposite side of the personality wheel. But larger and newer churches—and churches that wish to become that way—love pastors of this type, and vice versa.

So at a get-together of church planters and megachurch pastors (or their underlings, who are eager to become lead pastors themselves), they reinforce the image to one another. When they look across the table, they are often looking into a mirror. How could they *not* conclude, "This is what a successful leader looks like; this is how we do ministry"?

The stereotypical director loves getting things done. Maybe it is more accurate to say that they *hate* when things do *not* get done. Either way, they are very good at knocking out tasks. They also have a strong tendency to see everything—including ministry—in terms of tasks and accomplishment.

For many ministry staffs, achieving objectives and accomplishing tasks are the default mental model. Task accomplishment is the supreme value and the basis for praise and blame. Hiring personnel is itself just another task to complete, and a new staff member is just another cog in the ministry machine.

So when a leader on a staff like this talks to their team, they are almost always talking about tasks. *Did you send that email? Did you resolve that complaint?* But that should not be surprising. *What else are we here to do—that's why we call it "work," right?*

There is absolutely nothing wrong with this type of person being a pastor or any other kind of leader. (There had better not be—I, David, am this type.) But where this image is preferred, leaders who fit the mold are often allowed to take it to an extreme. Their strengths are rewarded: drive, grit, competitiveness, productivity. But their weaknesses are indulged, excused, and even justified: overbearing demeanor, workaholism, undisciplined anger, arrogance. In short, this kind of leader can be a real jerk and not know it. They might even be praised for it.

Systematic Management

Despite what we have said so far, many high-assertive, task-oriented lead pastors do have a way with people, especially if they were once church planters. They are often charismatic, sometimes magnetic. They are also entrepreneurial and even iconoclastic; they break the mold and make their own.

That style of ministry can be appealing, but as a church grows, something more is needed. Organizational energy must be harnessed and coordinated; order must be reestablished. The church needs reliable systems and rational management that the lead pastor is neither interested in nor able to provide.

Enter the executive pastor, and along with the XP enter axioms, structures, four-by-fours, processes, protocol, and data—more boxes to check.

Some churches excel at engineering ministry to the point that their peers look at them in awe. So do we, by the way—at a certain size, a church cannot function without such structural craftsmanship. But there is such a thing as overengineering, especially when it silently subtracts humanity from the equation. In time, overbuilt organizational architecture is revealed to be surprisingly brittle.

Scarce Care

The type of leadership we have been describing is heavy on accomplishment and light on relationship. Ironically, that kind of leadership is also *light on leadership*, because without relationship, you cannot lead anybody anywhere. This is especially true for younger generations, particularly when they do not feel appreciated.

Cue the sarcastic pantomime of someone pathetically playing a violin. And roll your eyes at the oversensitive millennials. But if you are married, think about your marriage for a moment. A marriage is not sustained by occasional grand gestures. If your marriage merely consists of you doing your thing, your spouse doing their thing, occasional "staff meetings" between the two of you, and doing something nice once in a great while, your marriage is not likely to last.

Yet that is how many leaders function with their teams. Their actions essentially say, "You do your thing; I do mine. I will give you the occasional attaboy, but I am never really going to know you, and for that matter, you will never really know me. Once a year I might give you a raise and maybe a gift card to Olive Garden. (See? I appreciate you!)"

Then they wonder why team members leave—and why they are left to deal with the headache of replacing key people.

The Cost of Common Leadership

If there is anything we have learned as staffing specialists, it is this: people quit managers much more often than they quit jobs. Let that sink in for a minute.

People occasionally do leave jobs for opportunities to do new and greater things. And sometimes people leave jobs for various family reasons. But people probably leave for reasons like these less often than you might think—especially when you are thinking about your own organization, where it is easiest for you to have blinders on. You know the reasons that departing staff have given you for leaving. But we want you to consider this question seriously: *What are your people silently telling you that they are not saying with words?*

It is a rare person who will be more loyal to their supervisor than their supervisor is to them. But think about what the common leadership model communicates to the people being led. It says, *I keep you here because you accomplish tasks. I keep you here because you help build me a big church. I keep you here because you make me money.* But conversely, it also says, *I don't keep you here because I care about you. I don't keep you here because I know your kids. I don't keep you here because I want you to flourish.* If no loyalty is communicated to your people, what will keep them loyal to you?

Make no mistake, there are plenty of reasons to leave. Job posts get circulated. Websites aggregate position openings. It takes only a few clicks for members of your team to picture

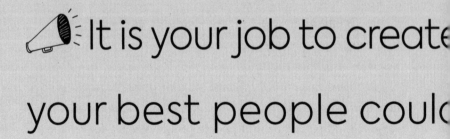

It is your job to create
your best people coulc

themselves somewhere else. Every day we see people leaving jobs to take the exact same job in a place that they hope is better than the place they came from.

On top of that, your best people are being approached directly by other organizations. When you have great people, others will try to recruit them. When others see talent, they want it on their team, and the church is no different. It is your job as a leader to keep them from going. It is your job to create an environment that your best people could not imagine leaving.

Do you work at it every day? Because there are heavy costs for neglecting that duty.

Counting the Cost

The common model of leadership incurs heavy opportunity costs—the chances a team misses because it is not as productive as it could be. But setting opportunity costs aside for the moment, look at the costs directly related to losing and replacing a staff member.

an environment that

not imagine leaving.

I (David) worked in a student ministries position for several years. At the peak of the ministry, my campus served 250 students a week. When I left that ministry for a new job, the church had an interim student ministries director as a stopgap for a year before they brought a new guy on board. When he took over, he had twelve students to work with. (You read that right.) Everything collapsed in the transition; there was no handoff of students, volunteers, or momentum. The new director was a gifted and hardworking individual, and he grew the ministry back to about 175 students. But it took him five years to do it.

Those lost years—not to mention the lost people—came in a situation where the church selected the *right* person to fill the open position. Now imagine what would have happened if they had hired the wrong one.

With a little effort, we can estimate the monetary cost of replacing a key staff member. If you hire a staffing agency to find an ideal candidate, that comes with a cost. It is increasingly common for larger churches to offer a signing bonus for upper-echelon positions, so add in another few thousand dollars for that. Do not forget a few grand for moving expenses. More importantly, add three to six months' worth of compensation because it will take that long for the new hire to learn enough and build enough rapport in their new position to start making the contributions you hired them to make. Then add in the monetary value of the time you and other staff had to redirect toward finding and hiring a new candidate and keeping things going in the absence of the person you lost. Finally, do not ignore the lost revenue from church members who were attached to the previous person and either left the church or scaled down their giving, not to mention the attrition caused by a struggling program, as was described in the example of David's departure.

All in all, how high can the tab run as the effects of the lost staff member and the new hire ripple through the organization? For a key position, a church can expect to spend tens of thousands of dollars to find a replacement for that hire. We would argue that in a small- to medium-size church, even though the absolute cost might be much lower, the cost as a percentage of the annual budget might be even greater than in a big church.

So if you have never considered it before, consider it now: if you succeed day in and day out at helping your people love their work, that could win you the greatest cost savings in your entire budget. On the other hand, if you neglect that task, you might play a part in incurring the largest unplanned expense of your organization—not once, but over and over again.

The Things That Are Beneath You

The staffing side of Slingshot Group regularly posts open ministry positions on social media. Once when we posted a position, a reader commented, "You mean there's no one in that church who wants that job? That's a red flag for me."

Now, we believe strongly in the value of what we do at Slingshot Group. We believe that even if the modern church were as healthy and godly as it could possibly be, there would *always* be times when it would be the right thing for a church to hire outside itself and for a leader to move from one church to another. We believe we do a superlative job of helping make that happen. Nevertheless, we have to admit that the commenter on our post has a point. Slingshot and similar firms exist because churches' current leaders do not meet their expectations for their next staff member or because none of them will take the job.

Why is that?

Many churches ask us to help them with their staffing needs because they have high turnover or because they cannot retain top talent. They want us to deliver them a new hire who will stanch the personnel bleeding. We can help them do that. But it often requires us to do more than just present a sterling candidate. It often requires us to ask, "Why do you go through a new staff member every two years?"

Patrick Lencioni calls organizational health—a minimum of infighting and a maximum of joy and productivity—the single greatest competitive advantage in business. He cites Southwest Airlines as a shining example. When Lencioni asked Herb Kelleher, Southwest's CEO, why more competitors do not copy them, Kelleher replied, "They think it is beneath them."[1]

We say to many lead and executive pastors, "The things you might think are beneath you have become the reasons you are facing your current problems."

As we said before, Slingshot Group was founded to build remarkable teams. Our staffing division makes that happen by bringing great people from one organization to another. But our coaching division addresses the same challenge from a different angle. In effect, we offer a preventive maintenance program for the problem of high turnover. We envision a transformed church where no leader changes organizations because they are running *from* anything but only because they are running *to* the next waypoint on their mission from God.

The things you might think are beneath you have become the reasons you are facing your current problems.

The Alternative: IMPROVleadership

For decades, I (Stan) have been coaching people to excel at what they do and to love it. But as Slingshot Group grew from one coach (me) to many, I needed to find a way to coach our coaches in coaching. My coaching skills had developed naturally over time, so it was a challenge to know how to foster those skills in others. I needed to leave a trail of footprints that others could follow.

Together with Will Mancini, Slingshot's senior leadership advisor, David and I defined a coaching model embodied in five competencies that could be transferred to others. Our coaches learned the model and used it in their talks with our clients—lead pastors, executive pastors, NextGen pastors, worship pastors, nonprofit leaders, and more—to help them thrive in ministry.

We were blown away when we saw joy, productivity, and staying power erupt in the lives of the people we were coaching. But we saw something even more surprising—something we never anticipated. Senior leaders—lead and executive pastors—asked us to teach them how to coach their people the way we had coached them. They wanted to see everyone on their staff love and excel in what they do. They caught a vision for what could happen if everyone experienced the kind of vocational, relational joy they had been feeling and how it could transform their churches and pour fuel onto their ministries.

So we trained senior leaders as if they were our coaches, and they coached their people. Ministry teams were transformed. Even leaders who worked together but could barely speak to each other began serving together as teammates.

Then we were invited to deliver the same coaching training to entire staffs so that they could coach their volunteers. The transformation that started in the life of one senior leader began penetrating and permeating a whole organization.

We saw that God was doing something. We realized that if all leaders adopted the competencies of coaches, the common model of leadership would be turned inside out. Precious resources would be saved. Productivity would soar. And the world would know that we are disciples of Jesus because we love one another (John 13:35).

So today we are sharing what we have learned with the world. We call it IMPROVleadership.

Loving People

IMPROVleadership can be summed up as a way of leading that treats your people like people, not merely as accomplishers of tasks. We know—you already treat your people like people. But the question is, do *they* know that?

My (Stan's) son Nate was a great baseball player as a teenager—a high school star who won a scholarship to play ball at a Division I college. Eighteen years later, Nate and I went to the Rose Bowl Game on New Year's Day, and we ran into one of my former work colleagues whom I had not seen in years (which is something of a miracle amid a hundred thousand people). The first words out of his mouth when he saw Nate—now in his forties—were, "Are you still playing baseball? Your dad used to talk about you all the time. He was so proud of you."

In that moment, two things happened. First, Nate felt loved. It was an out-of-the-blue reminder that I take so much joy in him and in what he does that I have to share it with other people.

The second thing was that *I* felt loved by my old friend. It showed me that when I had talked about my son years before, he took a keen interest in what mattered to me, so much so that he remembered it instantly many years later.

Here is the lesson: that moment might easily never have happened. I am not just talking about the coincidence of running into an old friend at the Rose Bowl; I mean the conversation that happened so naturally. I have always loved Nate, but he would not have been reminded I love him in that moment if I had not been in the habit of praising him to other people. My friend loved me, but I wouldn't have been reminded of it if he had not engaged with me about my life's unfolding story years before.

As with your children and your spouse, so with your team at work. It is not enough that *you* know you love them. It is not even enough that *they* know you love them. They have to *feel* you love them if they are going to give you their all for the long haul. As we said before, the love that your team feels within is the most powerful force in leadership. We did not make this up—we learned it from the Master.

Disciplemaking 101

Jesus had been healing people and proclaiming the kingdom for a long time—maybe two years—and had acquired a large number of disciples who followed him and learned from him. But one day, Jesus took his movement to a new level. He chose twelve men to be his staff and successors. He called them apostles (Luke 6:13).

Mark's Gospel describes this moment in a curious way, but it is so subtle that it is easy to miss: "He appointed twelve that they might be with him and that he might send them out to preach and to have authority to drive out demons" (3:14–15).

The most interesting—and convicting—words in this sentence are small, simple ones: *with him.*

Jesus appointed twelve that they might be with him. Grammatically, it is a complete thought. Jesus's first purpose for calling the Twelve was for them to be with him.

Yes, Jesus also appointed them that he might send them out to preach and to have authority to drive out demons. Yet that was Jesus's second purpose, not only grammatically and sequentially but logically. You cannot send someone *from* you unless they are *with* you first. The apostles could not really go *for* Jesus unless they had been *with* Jesus.

This pattern is basic to our entire faith. We do not get to be *with* God by doing things *for* God, which is the operating system underlying every religious impulse humans naturally have. Paul calls that principle "the elements of the world" (Galatians 4:3, 9; Colossians 2:8, 20 CSB).

That works-based mindset—*for* God, then *with* God—may be universal, but it is completely backward. Nothing we can do for God will ever qualify us to be with him. Rather, we get to be with him because he went to the nth degree to *be with us.* God the Son became incarnate to be with us; he died on the cross so we could be with him.

Because we can be *with* God through Christ, we are now finally in a position to do something *for* God. It is our delight, not just our duty.

This is not breaking news when it comes to our theology. We might even embrace it (perhaps with struggle) when it comes to our ministry. But does this idea ring true in our leadership?

Let us ask you something. When you hire someone to your staff, do you hire them first to do something *for* you, or first to be *with* you? Do you let yourself be with them? Even if you inherited your staff, the questions still apply. What are the proportions of "with" and "for" in your working relationships? Do both your words and your actions communicate to your team that you want them to be with you in a meaningful way?

This is how Jesus operated, and he set an example for us to follow. And we should want to follow it—after all, he did launch the greatest disciplemaking movement the world has ever seen. It is our job to continue it. At the end of the day, the principles of IMPROVleadership may simply be part of the syllabus of Disciplemaking 101.

Why People Stay

People are drawn to take a new position in a new organization for all kinds of reasons. They might relish the challenge. The position might allow them to focus more of their energies on what they do best. They might have a strong attraction to the location, or they might be eager for a step up in salary.

But the reasons for which people go to a new workplace are not usually the main reasons they stay there. Good people—people with the talent to go elsewhere—mainly stay in one place because people care about them, their supervisor most of all. It is because when they show up in the morning, they are not greeted first by action items but by active interest. It is because they are serving someone who knows them and their story. It is because they know that if they were ever to announce their resignation, their boss would be in their driveway within the hour, saying, "Let's talk," with genuine concern. Frankly, it is because they know someone gives a rip whether they work there or not.

At any given time, there may be people on your team whom you want to transition out. But what are you doing about the rest? Intellectual, data-based, process-oriented managerial advice is not going to solve this for you. But something else will: being in your people's lives and really understanding them. In other words, love they can feel.

CHAPTER 2

All Part of the Job

Why the Best Leaders
Learn to Improvise

Before we got into the coaching business, we were each in the music business—Stan as a producer and arranger and David as a lead singer in a series of bands before going into NextGen ministry. So we are well acquainted with improvisation (or "improv" for short). In music, improvisation means playing music that has not been scripted in advance but is developed on the fly. Because of our experience, however, we know that improv is not what most people think it is.

Most people think improvisation is making something up on the spot out of thin air. They also think the talent to do that is so magical that people who have it must be touched by angels—that what is impossible for the rest of us comes naturally to them.

Wrong.

We don't pretend that natural talent has nothing to do with it.

Some people have more to work with than others; it comes easier to some than others. But improv skills do not drop from the sky. What you hear and see onstage when someone is improvising is the result of a whole lot offstage that you never hear and see.

Improv is *not* making something up on the spot. Improv is bringing together many basic, well-known elements to form a complex whole that fits with the moment. An improvising musician usually follows a preset roadmap of which note combinations (chords) to strike in what order (a "progression") and which other notes sound harmonious or edgy when they are added in. Improvisers have short patterns of notes ("licks") that they have drilled into their fingers with hours of practice so that they can reproduce them without thinking, purely from muscle memory. They string these patterns together to make a melody. Improvisers also spend countless hours practicing with other musicians, learning to listen at the same time they are playing so that they cooperate as one part of a whole team. Finally, they have a persistent willingness to fail—to risk sounding bad, learn from it, practice more, and try again without being self-conscious.

When all these rudiments have been ingrained into a musician's experience over a long time, they can pull them up and put them together in a moment with a little conscious thought and a lot of unconscious action. That is how an improviser speaks beautiful, creative, expressive thoughts through their instrument.

You improvise too, hundreds of times every day. It is called language. But do you speak as beautifully as an improvising musician?

Are most of your conversations scripted? Actually, are *any* of them truly scripted, where everything you and the other person are going to say is set in advance, word for word? Unless you are a professional actor, we guess not. None of us consciously think about the vast majority of the words we say in day-to-day life. We have thoughts to convey, we open our mouths, and the words just spill out.

But the simplest, most routine sentence we utter rests on thousands of hours of experience learning words, grammar, and syntax. It comes by a little instruction and a lot of trial and error. We listened to others talk, engaged in conversation, made mistakes, learned, and tried again, much of it at such a young age that we can't even remember. We do not improvise with language because we are miraculously blessed—we improvise because we are humans who were raised by humans. We had to learn to improvise with language to survive.

Yet even now, there are times when we don't know what to say. We lack the words to get what we want, or the pattern of words we are accustomed to using keeps getting us what we do *not* want, but we struggle to find an alternative.

The level of difficulty rises when we are leaders, because our words have more power than ever before. We have more responsibility for what happens and does not happen as a result of what we say. Though we find ourselves in some situations where we have had a lot of practice and know what to do, we also find ourselves in situations where we haven't a clue. For example, we might feel great when it is our turn to command a room, but we don't know how to play a supporting role or collaborate with others well. Or we might know how to lead a planning meeting, but we don't know what to say to an employee whose husband announced that he is going to leave her.

IMPROVleadership is your invitation to go back to the practice room and drill new chords and new licks into your fingers to play in a new style when you need it. It gives you the ability to contribute to any situation, wherever you go. *You can learn this.*

As you work at it, you may find that the band around you has been trying to play a song the whole time, but they have been waiting for you to jump in and join them. You just never heard the music before.

Your Job Description

We invite you to learn how to improv because we would like for you to do your job. That might sound startling or even offensive, but walk with us for a minute, and let us show you what we mean.

Have you reviewed your job description lately? Maybe it is current, maybe not. Either way, use the blank space here to jot down the basics of your job from memory before reading ahead. (We are talking about four to six bullet points here, the high points—do not overthink this.)

MY JOB DESCRIPTION

....

....

....

....

....

....

....

Now consider this question: *Is raising your team's performance and productivity part of your job description?*

It might not stand alone as its own bullet point.

Is raising your team's performance and productivity part of your job description?

If not, that is fine, but we want to know whether the task of raising your team's performance is implied in what you *do* have written down. In other words, does your team need to perform at a high level for you to accomplish your job? Or is mediocre performance good enough?

If elevating your people's performance is part of your job description—whether explicitly or implicitly—then we have news for you: IMPROVleadership is part of your job description too because your improv skills raise the performance of the people you lead.

We are professional coaches, and years of experience have proven to us that IMPROVleadership really does raise the quality and quantity of the work of the people we coach.

If you supervise people, you are the on-site coach of your team. What would happen if you consciously made coaching an essential part of your job description?

Raise Productivity

People want to be known. *Your* people want to know that *you* know them. Few people want to be reduced to their job description (and if they do, watch out). Your people are individual people, and they want to be regarded as such. They also want to know *you*; they want you to be more than *your* job description.

Yet when people do not have confidence that their supervisor knows them as individuals, they tend to act guarded. People enter a workplace with all sorts of fears, including the fear of being judged, of being looked at a certain way, or of being marginalized in their role. Their guard is up to some degree. It might look different in different personalities, but everyone tends to hold something back—effort or cooperation or honesty or a request for help—while they sniff out whether they are in a secure situation.

In too many cases, people wisely conclude that they are not secure at work. Many supervisors manage by authority and fear, perhaps unknowingly. Yet all it takes for a person to close down is to get barked at for a mistake or snubbed for not speaking the right insider jargon or given short shrift when they raise a problem. When this happens, people conclude that they had better tread carefully. They stop communicating candidly, sharing information with colleagues, and asking questions. They hesitate before taking initiative, they lose their enthusiasm, and they waste time with distractions. When a worker takes this turn, their productivity plunges and the team's performance suffers.

Here is the important point: someday—maybe today—you *will* be short with someone who works for you. You will overlook someone. You will not take something as seriously as they think you ought to take it, or you will take something *too* seriously. This is inevitable. The question is, have you built up a continually replenished reservoir of goodwill and trust to keep the person engaged even when you disappoint them? And have you ever drawn out their best in the first place?

In general, a manager has something they are trying to get out the door—in Seth Godin's language, to "ship"—whether it is a physical product or a weekend worship service or whatever else. That product and all the steps and standards to ship it compose the manager's typical target.

Yet ironically, and contrary to what you might expect, mere single-minded focus on that target is *not* enough to achieve it. Or at least, it does not achieve it again and again over the long haul. When a manager doesn't treat their team as people—when they're treated as a set of tools to get a task done—then the team's performance will degrade over time. Milestones will get missed. People will leave, adding a burden on those who remain and levying a surcharge on the manager's time in the form of the effort needed to replace people. Morale drops, and turnover increases. A vicious spiral commences.

By the way, as we use the word *manager*, understand a concept embedded in it that we wish would vanish from leaders' thinking: *control*. Know this: people do not want to be managed. The idea of management is filled with fear. What we all want is to be led and to be developed.

In sum, when you consistently prioritize the target over the individual who works for you, you lose both. But on the flip side, when you prioritize the individual as highly as you do the target, you get both. When you drive hard to achieve objectives, you impair your ability to achieve them. Yet when you slow down enough to ask good questions of the people around you, as a skilled coach would—questions that show you really care about their past, present, and future—you get better results. Your people love their jobs more, and they love *you* more, so they work harder, better, and longer for you.

In the end you go further, faster. It sounds like a recipe for productivity to us.

Make Your Team into Your Dream Team

I (Stan) was in the music business for a long time, and I still keep a toe in it. I have learned that just as the average person does not know what it takes to improvise music, they also do not know what it takes to produce excellent music.

People put entirely too much weight on talent, but they

do not pay enough attention to what happens when the same team gets plenty of practice working together. We all know that the Beatles were talented. But most people do not know that when the Beatles came to America, they had already performed together twelve hundred times.[1]

This is relevant because when supervisors get frustrated with their teams, they frequently conclude that they have a talent deficit. They assume that the way to remedy the problem is to get new, different, better people. Too often they do not consider what would happen if they were to keep and coach the same group long enough to produce something really special.

We see this all the time in our work with ministry staffing. The average church gets excited by something "shiny"—a candidate with a résumé that includes *that* ministry. We mean the ministry with the big name, the big budget, the big attendance figures, the big conference, the big record deal. In other words, it is what the average ministry leader wishes their ministry was.

It is easy to fantasize about how amazing the staff at some other organization must be. It takes no work to see someone else's team as your dream team. Conversely, it takes a good deal of work to make your own team into a dream team. Yet it can be done. Certainly you may lack someone you need for a task sometimes, and sometimes a person you do have is not sufficient for their role and must be let go. But these situations don't come about as often as you think.

If you want, you can go out looking for a replacement x. But you can also coach your current x to be a better one. Both efforts take your time and your resources, and there are valid reasons for each. But have you considered the return you might get on your investment by coaching?

It takes no work to see someone else's team as your dream team. Conversely, it takes a good deal of work to make your own team into a dream team.

If your staff members came to your ministry with no desire to make it a stepping-stone to "that ministry," you have a huge asset on your hands. You have people who are not looking for eminence; they are looking for impact. They want to contribute, not get credit.

People like this are gold. When you know them, encourage them, train them, and inspire them, you help them become the best version of themselves. When you employ the competencies of coaching over time as an essential part of your job, you help your team blossom into all-stars.

Recruit without Recruiting

The power of coaching does not stop with your paid staff. It extends to your volunteers as well—perhaps even more so, since you cannot pay them in money. You can only pay them in love and significance.

When I (David) was in NextGen ministry, I had a classic problem: getting volunteers to serve in the student ministry. I tried everything I knew to fix the situation, but nothing seemed to work.

The turning point came when I stopped viewing the situation solely as a problem to fix and started viewing it as people to love. I realized that I had been inviting people to a task, but I was not inviting them into the students' stories or into my story—I did not ask them about their stories and weave them into *our* story. But after I started engaging relationally with potential volunteers and describing the opportunity in relational terms, I did not need to look for volunteers anymore. Volunteers came to me.

A skilled coach's relational competence draws people in. It also keeps the people you have; coaching combats the costs of staff turnover. Every organization has to fight to get and keep its best people; it is a part of your job. But fighting for your people becomes a lot easier if you fight every day.

How to Change Your Culture

So how do you go about creating a staff culture where talent flocks to you and where your best people stay long enough to make something great?

It is a tried-and-true principle: when you are a leader, the primary way you develop a culture is by developing yourself. You are not above the system you lead; you are an integral part of it. In fact, despite how it may feel some days, you are a highly influential part of it.

This may not ring true to you; you may sometimes feel frustrated by the way other people resist your efforts. But that frustration belies your real power.

Alexander Calder was one of the great American artists of the twentieth century. He is best known for sculpting gigantic mobiles that look like elegantly simple versions of the toy that dangles over a baby's crib. Calder's mobiles are composed of sheet-metal "sails" hanging from long, arcing metal rods. The rods in turn dangle from each other like branches, and the whole complex is suspended from the ceiling by one wire.

Calder's largest works weigh as much as half a ton, yet they are so perfectly balanced that they rotate on the gentle currents of a gallery's air-conditioning. But if you were to move just one piece of sheet metal to a different position, the entire piece would droop awkwardly, and the mobile would stop revolving.

Calder's mobiles teach a great lesson of leadership. Every

leader of a team thinks of themselves as the sculptor of a mobile: they have the job of arranging all the pieces into something that works. There is some truth to that, but there is a big deception there too. A sculptor is not a part of the work he makes, but you are a part of your team. Actually, most days you are less the sculptor of your team than you are a piece of sheet metal hanging in it.

But do not let this discourage you, because you happen to be an exceptionally weighty piece! If you change your position in the mobile, your shift changes the whole shape of your team. Trying to change other people on your team is often frustrating and exhausting. But you can exercise an enormous amount of leverage in your team by changing yourself. In fact, changing yourself changes the whole system whether the system likes it or not.

When you add coaching to your job description and start practicing it, that act alone starts changing your team even before your people respond to what you are coaching them to do. It is natural for supervisors to pick up coaching as if it were one more weapon in their arsenal to aim at people to get them to do what the manager wants. But we are saying that coaching does not start working by changing your people—it starts working by changing you, and *that* changes your people.

Curiosity

When Will Mancini worked with us to develop IMPROV leadership, he kept defining it as getting to both the heart of the matter and the heart of the person you are leading. Anytime you are not engaging those two "hearts" in an interaction with someone, you are not in the sweet spot of the moment.

Many leaders have only "the heart of the matter" on their mind when they look at their people. But leaders who use IMPROVleadership look for more. They have one hard-to-come-by character trait that underlies all effective coaching and leadership: curiosity.

To be effective as a coach, you must be genuinely curious about who your people are—what their life has been like so far, what it is like now, and where it may be going in the future. Curiosity drives you to ask good questions, and questions not only gather valuable information but often shape people's behavior more powerfully than your statements do. Above all, when you lean in by showing curiosity about someone on your team, they lean in by attending more closely to you and to the work they do for you.

This is all well and good, but it may also be discouraging. It is not easy for a leader to admit to themselves that they are not all that curious about the lives of the people on their staff. But it is even harder when it seems there is nothing they can do about it. Trying to get yourself to "be more curious" might seem like trying to get yourself to grow an inch taller or to enjoy eating beets.

But that is not actually so. You *can* grow in curiosity about your people. The key is to practice the five competencies of IMPROVleadership. These competencies are the skills that good coaches use to bring out the best in people, but practicing them also brings out the best in the coach. Over time, these competencies make curiosity come naturally. Eventually, the experienced coach looks at people in a new way—they see every person as a fascinating treasure of significance and destiny.

Can you imagine how you would work if you knew that your

supervisor saw *you* that way? Now imagine your staff working that way for you.

On-the-Job Training

The rest of this book is devoted to teaching and illustrating the five competencies of coaching, IMPROVleadership-style, with practical tools to make them real in your leadership. This book does not instruct the reader in everything that is necessary for good leadership because if you care enough about your leadership to pick up this book, we are confident that you are already a highly capable leader. Of course leadership requires technical proficiency in the area you lead. And of course it requires vision and the ability to communicate future direction compellingly. You already know this. In fact, the "common leader" we described in the previous chapter knows it too and is usually quite adept in these areas. IMPROVleadership is not a replacement for these qualities; it is a complement to them. It is an approach to leadership from a totally different angle— coaching—that many leaders are missing.

Earlier in this chapter we invited you to take stock of your job description, and we made the case that coaching your team should be part of it. Too often, as leaders, we treat the "soft skills" of relational investment as optional, as a cherry garnish on top of an already adequate manager. But what if they are not optional? What if they were required as part of your job description? How different would you be as a leader if you believed that your ability to coach was essential to what you were hired to do—that your job depended on it?

Now imagine what would happen in your organization if

How different would you be as a leader if you believed that your ability to coach was essential to what you were hired to do—that your job depended on it?

you and the leaders around you put coaching competencies into practice. As we mentioned previously, Herb Kelleher of Southwest Airlines said many organizations do not move forward because they believe that learning these skills is beneath them. Compare his observation with what Paul says about love in 1 Corinthians 13. Paul could have been an elite performer, he could have had unparalleled knowledge and vision, and he could have worked more devotedly than anybody else—all excellent attributes—but if he didn't demonstrate love to the people he led, his leadership would have been a zero. The simplest ingredient is the most overlooked and also the most important.

No matter what problem you might encounter in your organization, you have a better chance of navigating it successfully with IMPROVleadership. This is what we want you to hear: *you can learn how to improv.* It does not matter how much natural talent you have. It does not matter whether you are a "people person." On a coaching scale of one to ten, if you are a two, you can become a five; if you are a five, you can become an eight. You can grow, and growth happens when you practice these competencies. We wrote this book to show you how.

CHAPTER 3

Story Mining

The Beginning of Coaching Is Knowing Your Players

When a woman we'll call Cristina joined a team I (David) led, she had already walked through an incredible story of sorrow, pain, redemption, and joy. Like many couples, Cristina and her husband had walked for years down the path of infertility. Infertility is an intimate form of suffering that is often difficult for other people to understand and appreciate. Mere small talk about families can ignorantly rub at the sensitive wound. Because Cristina worked on a church staff for over ten years, families were a constant topic of conversation. She kept a stiff upper lip, yet she longingly prayed for a child of her own, and she asked her colleagues to pray with her as well.

Years passed, and Cristina and her husband made the big and challenging commitment to adopt two siblings. Their new children filled them with joy and were cause for celebration in their circle of relationships. But that was not all. As Cristina and her husband settled in to being parents, she became pregnant! Nine months later, Cristina gave birth to their third child. The situation was simply astounding, as if a biblical miracle had dropped into the middle of this church staff.

I was blown away by Cristina's story when I brought her on board my team. A few weeks later, while I was talking with Cristina, I happened to mention her third child by name.

Cristina stopped, stunned. Then she cried. *Uh-oh*, I thought. *What did I do?*

"David, I'm sorry—I'm just in shock that you said that," Cristina said tearfully. "See, I always had a good relationship with the lead pastor I served under at my former church. We worked well together for many years. But he could never remember my child's name."

Whoa.

Before I go one sentence further, I want you to know that I could absolutely be that lead pastor myself. I am not naturally "good with names," and I am not naturally overflowing with interest in the details of people's lives. In general, we all remember what is most important to us, and if I did what came naturally to me, other people's kids' names would not qualify for rapid recall. In the past, I might have believed I cared about my staff, but my memory would have shown that I was much more interested in what they did at work than in who they were at home.

The reason I knew Cristina's child's name wasn't because I'm such a swell guy or naturally gifted. It is because over time, I have learned a skill that did not come naturally, but I have been practicing it for long enough that it is becoming second nature. I have made a habit out of the first competency of IMPROVleadership. We call it *Story Mining*.

What Is Story Mining?

Story Mining is *thoughtfully uncovering a person's story and allowing it to shape the way you lead them.* When one of us gets a new client to coach, we always begin by getting to know the person. Critically, we want to get to know the person first *as a person*, not as a worker.

We mine for a person's story by asking them great questions at the right time to draw them out of themselves. We do not ask them questions as a setup to give them a task to do. We do not ask questions to analyze or diagnose them. We do not even ask questions to get them to imagine their future. (We will talk about this other important use of questions in a later chapter.) In short, Story Mining is not about making people better. It is about making people feel known.

What we learn about a person from Story Mining has value unto itself because the person has value unto themselves. If we do not have ulterior motives for our questions, our sincerity comes through. Our curiosity demonstrates that we view the person as a unique, interesting, valuable human being—as someone who *matters to us* aside from anything they might do for us, as someone who is more than their job description and more than their output.

You can compare Story Mining to the opening scene of a movie. Imagine a wide-angle shot of Paris on a cool, cloudy day. You see stately buildings along the Seine and taxis moving along the riverside. The camera gradually zooms in to traffic crossing a bridge. The angle narrows further to the pedestrians walking on the bridge, and you see one person coming into focus in the center of the frame. He is standing along the rail, looking out at the river. The angle gets tighter and tighter, excluding all other figures, until the frame is filled with the man's face and the far-off expression in his eyes.

Story Mining is like this. It starts with a broad view and general understanding, but with patient, thoughtful, inviting questions, you zoom in to the heart of the person you are coaching—or rather, they open up and share themselves with you.

Another way to imagine Story Mining is as if you are following tracks in the woods in hopes of spotting rare wildlife. Each good question reveals more of the marks on a winding forest trail. Eventually you reach a still pool where the animal is silently waiting. The pool represents the deep well of thought and emotion in a person's life—the source of what they do, what they will not do, and why.

Setting Up Instruction

When you use Story Mining to coach your team, it enhances your leadership in two ways.

First, Story Mining **sets up instruction**. Story Mining makes people on your team feel that their workplace is a safe environment. It helps them get comfortable with their coworkers and fosters cooperation and collaboration (as we will illustrate below). Yet it also helps them get comfortable with you as their supervisor, and it opens them up to more coaching. Skillfully using Story Mining wins you permission to use the other competencies of IMPROVleadership.

Think about parenting as an example. Conventional wisdom says that you cannot effectively parent all your children the same way, and that axiom happens to be correct. Yet we commonly lapse into a posture of parenting children as if they were alike ("I let her have this, so I guess I'll let you have it too.") In the short run, it seems "easier" to parent that way, but it is not as effective as when we think carefully about what connects best with each child.

Leadership at work is the same as leadership at home. It may seem easier to lead everyone as if they were alike—indeed, both children and team members may demand it of us!—but it is not as effective. Good leadership recognizes the differences among people—what draws them in and what pushes them away, where they are at their best and where they aren't. But you can lead people effectively only if you know them individually.

I (David) once took a class on how to supervise people to prevent burnout. One question we discussed was how long a workweek should be—in other words, we talked about how many hours a person can work over the long haul without getting burned out. In my view, that is the wrong question because it assumes that there is one answer for everyone. In reality, one person is burned out by working a certain number of hours per week, but that same workweek fuels someone else. One person receives an out-of-the-blue day off as a reward; another takes it as a rebuke, a sign that their work is not valuable. One person takes a certain amount of time to perform a task; another does it in half the time, so making them work the same length of time as the first person penalizes them for their efficiency. Rather than dignifying people by treating them "fairly," standardization can be punitive because it does not take into account their unique makeup and history. Story Mining is the way to learn these important differences between people and supervise them accordingly.

As we said earlier, Story Mining does not work if you ask a person questions about their life and then immediately exploit their answers to leverage them toward tasks and outputs. It will be obvious to them that you did not really want to know them: you wanted to manipulate them. But what they share one day can indeed become valuable in a directive conversation later. In the weeks or months that follow, your grasp of a person's story may be a critical bridge to give them practical instruction in a form you know they will understand and take to heart.

Stimulating Production

The second leadership benefit of Story Mining is that it **stimulates production**. This benefit comes about entirely indirectly, but it is very real.

When I (David) was on staff at Parkcrest Christian Church, my senior pastor, Mike Goldsworthy, consistently made time for us to connect as people. Often when you meet with your supervisor, the main question you are being asked is "What have you accomplished?" But in my meetings with Mike, the first questions were always "Who are you?" and "How are you?" *then* "What have you accomplished?" I knew he knew me. While other supervisors I worked for saw me as someone to accomplish tasks for them, Mike saw me as a person.

At Slingshot, Stan shows people the same kind of love. Because we know that Stan knows us, we work harder for him. Because he takes the time to show us that he cares about us, we want to impress him more because the desire to be known and understood is hardwired into all of us. Stan is more keenly interested in us than he is in our output, and that increases our output.

Stan gets the best out of his people. Of course, he knows

this, and I know he knows it, but that does not detract from its power. I know that Stan's interest in me draws more productivity out of me, but I also know he has a bigger reason for showing interest. He shows interest because he finds me interesting—he is curious.

Why We Don't Ask Questions

Peter Drucker famously said, "The leader of the past knew how to tell. The leader of the future will know how to ask."[1]

Drucker uttered that oft-quoted statement a good thirty years ago. So has the future come yet or what? Why is it that more leaders do not apply Drucker's dictum?

The answer is simple: fear.

For starters, leaders don't ask people questions about their lives because they are **afraid they don't have time for it**.

Doing Story Mining well takes time and attention. You have to be present in the moment. You have to stop what you are doing. You cannot look over the person's shoulder; you cannot glance at your watch; you cannot nod while redirecting your thoughts to the next thing you have to do or how you are going to get the meeting back on track.

It is common to shove a crumb of humanity into a meeting by asking, "How was your weekend?" and hoping for a bland response. But to stop someone in the hallway to show keen interest in their weekend, their kids, or their past takes a different level of curiosity and investment.

Another reason leaders do not ask questions is that they are **afraid of irritating the other people in the room** by slowing everything down.

Many of us were perversely trained in school not to ask too many questions. Maybe you can remember a time when the whole class understood the lesson (or acted like they did), but you did not get it. You bravely put up your hand and asked a question. You did not understand the answer, so you asked a follow-up. By your third question, you still didn't grasp it, and your classmates muttered or even jumped in to "help" you, not because they cared but because they were annoyed. Eventually, whether you understood or not, you shut your mouth and hoped you could figure it out later. The lesson you came away with had nothing to do with what the instructor was trying to teach; rather, you learned that you mustn't hold up everyone else by asking questions.

Many of us brought this lesson with us to the workplace. There it was reinforced by managers who looked at us suspiciously or even rebuked us for asking questions. Questions were viewed as the mark of someone who was not "all in," who was not on board with the program. So we learned to keep our questions to ourselves because we were **afraid of being seen as a troublemaker**.

In stark contrast, I (David) always find it fascinating watching Stan in a meeting. Stan will pause what we are working on to ask someone a deep, evocative, personal question. Then he asks a follow-up question. Then another. By this time, people are starting to get uncomfortable. (Heck, *I'm* getting uncomfortable.) But Stan keeps it up regardless of whether people are shifting in their seats. He does this in part to communicate that we always have time for each other as people. Stan knows that he has not hired people who want to shirk their jobs—stuff will still get done. But he always wants us to prioritize each other as human beings, and he doesn't care how uneasy that makes the task-oriented people in the room.

There are still more reasons we don't ask questions. Once again, many of us learned in school that we are supposed to have all the answers, and the teacher (the leader) *definitely* has all the answers. We don't ask questions when we become leaders because we are **afraid of looking dumb**. That certainly has been the case for me. I always thought that not asking questions was a sign of strength and intelligence; it showed I was ahead of the game. I would try to figure things out before I would lower myself to ask a question. My problem was pride, and unfortunately, *that* was what came across to others, not my intelligence.

Even worse, when it comes to details about people's personal lives, we may not ask because we believe we should already know. (And maybe we are right.) We realize that we really should know our coworker's daughter's name by now, and it is too late to ask. And if we ask personal questions about other things, who knows how we might embarrass ourselves? The last thing we want is to reveal our ignorance or stumble into a taboo topic. In short, we are **afraid of looking like a jerk** who doesn't know their team.

The awkwardness that comes from not knowing something about a coworker that you should know is a common problem, and before this chapter ends, we're going to give you a few hacks to overcome it. But first, take a moment to assess your knowledge of your staff. How well do you know their stories?

HOW WELL DO YOU KNOW YOUR TEAM?

Answer for each person who reports to you directly.

1. What are your team member's children's names? Grandchildren's? (For bonus points, how old are they, or what grade are they in?)

....

....

....

2. Where and how did your team member meet his/her spouse?

....

....

....

3. Where did your team member grow up? How often do they go back there?

....

....

....

4. Where else has your team member lived that had a significant impact on their life story?

....

....

....

5. What is your team member's prized possession?

....

....

....

6. What (outside of work) does your team member enjoy doing?

....

....

....

7. What is your team member's idea of a great vacation?

....

....

....

How did you do?

The Power of Questions

God is unafraid of losing face or people's approval. Maybe that is why he is not afraid to ask questions.

When Adam and Eve disobeyed him, God responded by asking questions: "Where are you? . . . Who told you that you were naked? . . . What is this you have done?" (Genesis 3:9, 11, 13).

Jesus was a famous question-asker. The Gospels record 307 questions that Jesus asked.[2] Some of the most interesting include: "Do you want to get well?" (John 5:6), "Who do you say I am?" (Mark 8:29), and "Why do you call me good?" (Mark 10:18).

We are not the first to point this out, but it is interesting that a God who knows everything would ask people questions. God must see value in asking for the sake of the person hearing the question and also for the sake of his relationship with that person. (Note that after God asks a question, unless it is rhetorical, he waits to hear what the other person has to say. Unlike many people, God does not ask a question so he can answer it first, even though he has all the answers already.) Asking questions doesn't show stupidity; it reveals intelligence. Even more, it shows that we believe that the person we are asking a question of is valuable.

Chip Conley says, "A great question leads to a quest."[3] To restate what we have said repeatedly, questions are the natural outgrowth of curiosity—they only work when you care about the answer. When we ask a question, we go on a hunt for something interesting in someone's story. And the better the questions we ask, the more we find.

Curiosity

To get into Story Mining, start by considering yourself an active participant in the stories of the people around you. Recognize that just by knowing someone, you have become a character in their life story. You are not the most important character, however—their story is not about you. So you had better get to know the story in which you just appeared: who the other characters are and where the plot is going.

Cultivate a generalist's curiosity even if you have a specialist's role. While it is often valuable for a person to specialize in what they do, Story Mining requires a generalist's wide-ranging interest in all kinds of things, because you never know what is important to the person you are talking to and where you might find common ground.

My (Stan's) curiosity has a funny way of popping up in the oddest places and times. My family walked through a crisis when my grandson needed open-heart surgery. So my wife, Connie, and I traveled to be with our kids at the famous Boston Children's Hospital. The day after the operation, I had the great opportunity to ask the surgeon a question. (I waited for just the right moment: when asking great questions, timing is everything.)

My question caught the surgeon by surprise. Every day as she meets with families, she gets questions about her patients, about the success of the operation, about the prognosis for recovery, and about what to expect next. But that day I asked her a question about her team: "What caused this team to become world-renowned?" (I could not help myself—I was curious.)

She paused for a moment, then answered, "We've had the same nine doctors together for twelve years. So when we do what we do, we aren't guessing—it's like math to us. It's about teamwork and skill."

For me, having curiosity like this—whether about a world-class pediatric heart surgeon, a member of my staff, or a perfect stranger—comes naturally. It may not come so naturally to you, but that is all right. As we said in the last chapter, you can grow in Story Mining by intentionally applying yourself.

So let us ask you a question: What would you do differently if you were a professional question-asker? Because we propose that if you are a leader, you already *are* a professional question-asker by virtue of your leadership role.

Good Questions

Maybe you have heard the saying attributed to Albert Einstein: "If I had an hour to solve a problem and my life depended on the solution, I would spend the first fifty-five minutes determining the proper question to ask, for once I know the proper question, I could solve the problem in less than five minutes." We love this saying because it highlights the unsurpassed value of a great question.

Asking good questions is an art that is honed with practice. Small changes in wording can have a great effect. For instance, one of our favorite questions to ask the people we coach is "What are you interested in?" We love this question because we find that when we know what someone is interested in, we have a clue as to how we might impact their life.

But we never ask that question exactly that way. Instead, we ask, "What are you *keenly* interested in?" That little word *keenly* makes all the difference. It is the point at the end of the spear. It makes the hearer pause, sit up, take notice, and give a deep, thoughtful answer. With practice, you too will find little words that make a big difference in drawing out someone's story.

Remember, Story Mining starts broad and zooms in. You can (and in a new relationship, you should) start with the biographical basics. But as you zoom inward—or when you are talking with a person you have been leading for a while—you start to ask questions that are still open-ended but far more savory.

We love exercising our creativity to devise questions that draw out people's stories, and we would be delighted if you did the same. That said, there is no need to reinvent the wheel. Skilled coaches have developed and employed hundreds of great questions. Will Mancini told us that he is always on the hunt for great questions. In fact, he told us that he will buy an entire book of questions just to find one that he has never heard before. He considers himself a curator of questions.

That got us thinking that maybe we should help you start your own curated list of questions by sharing fifteen of our favorites.

15 GREAT STORY-MINING QUESTIONS

1. If you woke up in the morning and everything was "the way it should be," what changed?
2. Why did you want your current role when you started? Does this still ring true?
3. What is one mistake you've seen leaders make that you are determined never to make?
4. Do you feel you are known the way you'd like to be known?
5. What is the most embarrassing moment of your life?
6. How has your life been different from what you imagined?
7. Whom have you significantly influenced? How?
8. Who has been the most important person in your life?
9. What funny stories does your family tell about you?
10. What three skills are the most important to be a good parent?
11. As you consider the people in your life who have inspired you, what do you admire the most about them?
12. If you could wake up tomorrow having gained one quality or ability, what would it be?
13. When was the last time you read a book written from a perspective you disagreed with?
14. What is happening in your organization that would not happen if you were not there?
15. What are you most proud of?

Which question of our fifteen do you wish someone would ask you? Who on your team wants you to ask that question of them?

Story Mining in Real Time

All the competencies of IMPROVleadership, Story Mining included, are skills you can learn. Here are some practical training tools to help you acquire this leadership competency and coach your people like a pro. Remember, the more deliberately you practice, the more it becomes second nature and the better you will get.

Prepare to Question

First off, like our friend Will Mancini, **become a curator of questions**. As we said, you can literally buy whole books full of them. Never rest with the questions you have; always be on the lookout for new ones.

When you have an appointment coming up where you know you are going to be around people—a meeting, a sales call, a networking function—**prepare questions in advance**. You know you are going to end up in small talk with somebody before the appointment starts anyway. With a few moments' preparation, you could make it the best small talk that person has ever had, and you will gain precious understanding of that person's story.

Become a curator of questions.

Nevertheless, you cannot always prepare specially for each interaction because such moments often spring up when you are not expecting them. A vast storehouse of questions is a bit impractical in those situations—you cannot easily run away from a live conversation to retrieve your questions and then jump back in.

So **memorize three "back pocket" questions**. These are your go-to questions that are adaptable to all kinds of situations, so you can deploy them at a moment's notice. (Remember, this is all about how to improv—how to take the rudiments you have drilled into memory and put them together on the fly.) Pick three questions you like and then rotate new ones in as you gain experience.

At the time of writing, the three questions I (David) have in my back pocket include number one and number fourteen in this chapter's list. The third is, "If you were the coach, what would you say?" (I love that one—they never see it coming.)

We hope you are getting excited about the possibilities of asking great questions. But do not neglect the quality control step. **Answer your own questions before you ask others**. When you do so, you sometimes find that a question is not as clear as you thought it was. **Consider the timing or context of your situation.** A question might be good when a person has time to ponder it but not on the fly. **Also consider your relationship with the person you're asking.** A question may be good when you have already established deep rapport but not early in a relationship.

First Steps in Story Mining

Maybe you're ready to leave your desk, walk down the hall, and ask a good question. Prove you're prepared by **asking questions**

of children. Children make for a great laboratory to gauge your readiness. They do not pass judgment on you, yet they have a remarkable way of showing you whether your questions are good or bad, because they have no interest in keeping a conversation going just to make you feel comfortable. If you ask an unclear or overly complicated question, they will shrug. If you ask a question that requires no imagination, they will give you the most boring answer possible. But when you ask a good question about their world, they will reveal all sorts of things you never would have guessed. Asking a kid a good question puts the engine in their little heart and mind into overdrive. If you can ask a question that works well with a child, you're ready to ask a good question of an adult.

Speaking of children, one of the best ways to do Story Mining is to get people talking about their children. To start a recent executive team meeting at Slingshot, I (Stan) gave this instruction: "Take a few minutes to **brag about your family.**" We went around the room, and everyone bragged. I insisted on hearing every family member's name, and another team member wrote them down so that I had a record to study and follow up on later.

This exercise was good not only because it helped me learn people's stories. It also helped *them* learn one another's stories. It strengthened their appreciation of one another. You might wonder whether people tried to one-up each other as in obnoxious Christmas letters. To the contrary, permission to brag about their families made people too happy to be proud in the bad way. Joy bubbled up in the room, and it injected terrific energy and collaboration into the following agenda items of our meeting.

Do not confine your Story Mining to the expected small-talk

situations such as the moments before a meeting starts, however. The bonding power of Story Mining multiplies massively when you **do it on its own time for its own sake**.

Think about what you typically say to someone if you stop them in the hallway: "Hey, I need your help with something." "How's the project coming?" "Would you send me that report?" Now imagine what would happen if you stopped someone in the hallway and said, "Hey, do you have a second? I wanted to ask you something I've been asking some people lately: Who has been the most important person in your life?"

After they get over the shock, they will probably answer your question. Then they will ask you a question of their own: "Why did you want to know?"

"Oh, no reason in particular," you reply with a smile. "I just wanted to get to know you better." Mic drop.

Now, you may have realized that Story Mining is not a time-neutral activity. It has great benefits, but it carries a cost, and you will not get good at Story Mining until you are willing to pay the cost.

When people meet for a professional lunch, they commonly book an hour for it. When I (Stan) go out for lunch, I book an hour and a half. It takes me that long to accomplish what I want—that is, for the reason we planned to meet and also for Story Mining. If you want to get serious about knowing people, you need to **schedule appointments that are long enough to do it**.

Worth a Thousand Words: The Six-Sketch Storyboard

Story Mining consists of good questions, but there is more than one way to get good answers. We are generally accustomed to people answering questions orally and occasionally in writing, but there is another way people can answer as well: drawing. Drawing activates a different part of the brain than speaking or writing, so it often produces answers of a quality you do not get any other way.

One of our favorite coaching tools at Slingshot Group is the **Six-Sketch Storyboard.** Physically it is easy to construct—you can use anything from a napkin to a sheet of copy paper to a whiteboard. All you need to do is divide it into six boxes for six sketches.

The question we commonly ask our clients with the Six-Sketch Storyboard is "What moments have made you the leader you are today?" (You can also replace the word *leader* with a different one: *parent, person, Christian,* etc.) We direct the person

Figure 1: Stan's Six-Sketch Storyboard

we're coaching to select the six events from their life that have shaped their leadership most powerfully and then draw a simple sketch of each without using words.

We never cease to be amazed by what we learn of people's stories through this exercise. We are also amazed by the power of the Six-Sketch Storyboard to catalyze healing, reconciliation, and cooperation in a conflicted team, even one where staff members hardly speak to one another.

I (David) once led an IMPROVleadership staff training day with a nonprofit that had that problem. Three senior leaders were angling for resources, and the conflict made for a severe drag on the whole leadership team's efforts. So I led the team through the Six-Sketch Storyboard exercise, and I called on these three leaders to share their storyboards with the group one by one.

Each leader showed the sketches on their storyboard and described the events depicted on it. As their stories unfolded, these three conflicted leaders started seeing each other as human, maybe for the first time. Their stories were so moving and so engaging that the other twelve people in the room eagerly asked if they could share their storyboards too. My agenda came to a complete halt as this team told each other their stories, one after another. Some of them cried. Humanity entered the room.

When everyone had presented their storyboard, I asked the team, "Did you learn anything new about anyone in this room?" Every single person did. This was a team that had been together for a long time; the last person to join it had been there for five years already. But the whole dynamic changed once they knew each other's stories. The difference in what we were able to do after that storyboarding session was like night and day.

Story Mining with an Established Team

Story Mining is always easier when you are bringing on a new hire. It lends itself to the built-in get-to-know-you period. So if your people have been with you for a good while, as was the case for the nonprofit we just told you about, Story Mining could be trickier. You might feel awkward and uncomfortable launching into it out of the blue. That is no reason not to do it, but some tips can make it smoother.

For starters, accept the reality that you are going to have to **shake things up with your staff** if you have been together for a long time. Incremental adjustments will not help much because everybody mistakenly thinks they know each other's stories already.

The Six-Sketch Storyboard is a powerful tool to change that. Do it yourself on your own, and practice by sharing your storyboard with your spouse or a close friend. Then lead a meeting devoted to the exercise—maybe in a room you don't normally meet in—and share your storyboard before you have everyone else draw theirs.

Other exercises can accomplish something similar. For instance, send everyone to a different room and give them fifteen minutes to ponder two questions: "What was the happiest moment of your life?" and "What is the most difficult thing you ever accomplished?" Then bring them back together and take turns sharing and listening.

Another problem can arise when you are Story Mining with an established team. Sometimes basic biographical data has eluded your grasp, and it seems embarrassing for you to ask about it. This can arise in the Story Mining process itself. You ask a question, and a person begins talking about themselves in a way that assumes that you know information about them that you cannot recall. What do you do?

A common approach is to nod yes as if you know what they are talking about, then ask around and try to get the skinny on the situation later. While this is sometimes appropriate, it is not always the right move. Interrupting to ask a clarifying question may not hurt their feelings, even if it makes you feel a little foolish for a moment. In fact, they may appreciate your engagement and interest.

But some situations where you ask about something you should already know *will* cause offense. I know I (David) have been in those situations. Names of kids are an easy place for me to mess up, so sometimes I have had to **find creative workarounds** to get names back on my tongue.

In one meeting I asked a staff member to share a story about her kids with the whole team. I was careful to write down the names, and I have never forgotten them since. Another time I remembered the kids' names but could not remember which one was which. It was a small-talk situation with a bunch of people around, so I excused myself, barricaded myself in a bathroom, and did some rapid social media research to get the answer.

I have to be honest—I feel a little goofy admitting these stories. But I tell them to illustrate how important it is that you know your people personally. It does not pay off to avoid situations where you might look stupid. It is not justified to remain content with generalities ("How are the kids?" instead of "How is Jonathan?"). Specificity matters. Intimacy matters. Whether or not you have a naturally sticky memory does not matter. To get the most from your people over the long haul, you need to be as innovative, intentional, and willing to risk mistakes when it comes to their personal stories as you are when pursuing the most important metrics to your organization.

Developing a Culture of Curiosity

When you get the hang of Story Mining, it will begin to transform your team. When *they* get the hang of Story Mining, it will begin to transform your whole organization.

For instance, when I (David) was a student pastor, I had a plan for what our small groups were supposed to be doing in a given week or month. But I reminded my small group leaders that they knew the students in their groups better than I did. If they needed to put off my plan because of what they saw emerging in their group one week, they always had permission to do that. I was happy to **entrust leaders with freedom** because I knew they had mined for the stories of the students in their care and could skillfully steer their group in the direction it needed to go.

When you get the hang o

transform your team. When *the*

it will begin to transform

Leaders are conditioned always to give answers, not to ask questions. But you can change that in yourself and in the people who report to you. Imagine buying four fifty-dollar gift cards for your staff every month and using them to **reward the best question** asked in each weekly staff meeting. What is celebrated is repeated. Do you think that would increase the quantity and quality of good questions in your organization?

The right question is powerful enough to reshape time itself. In an instant, the clock seems to stop, yet your relationship with your team leaps years ahead, and so does your team's power.

So don't settle for telling and answering—strive to be asking. And don't settle for being a good question-asker—strive to become a professional question-asker. We have said it before, and we will say it again: make it your job to know your team's stories. Story Mining is optional if your people are disposable or if your relationship is purely transactional. But it is not optional if you want your people to love their work.

tory Mining, it will begin to

get the hang of Story Mining,

your whole organization.

CHAPTER 4

Precision Praising

Going beyond "Good Job" to Bring Out People's Best

As I (Stan) mentioned earlier, I have spent much of my career working as a music producer. I take the ear and the eye I developed in the music industry everywhere I go. So I noticed around 2014 when the ratings of the hit TV show *American Idol* dipped under the popularity of *The Voice*.

On the surface, the two shows have a lot in common: amateur hopefuls, live performances, belty solos, a cast of celebrities, and dramatic lighting. So why did *American Idol* eventually drop off the air for a season while *The Voice* kept going strong? I think it is because people do not want to be judged, like the contestants on *American Idol*. They want to be coached, like the contestants on *The Voice*.

In the same way, the people on your team do not want to be judged. They want to be coached. They want to be led and developed.

Coaches correct, but they also praise. (In fact, the best coaches praise so skillfully that they can often correct their team just by praising them. Sound crazy? In this chapter we will prove it to you.)

But that kind of praise is more than just being nice. And it does not mean dropping trite compliments or insincere flattery. The kind of praise we are talking about is the second competency of IMPROVleadership. We call it *Precision Praising*.

As a leader, you might not think praising people on your team is a mandatory part of your job, especially when they don't do anything to blow you away. But if it is your job to make your team better the way a coach does, you will find that Precision Praising is essential, and you will find opportunities to use it every day.

Wired for Praise

Precision Praising is *carefully crafting praise to inspire and course-correct your team*. It refers to the right words of affirmation given to the right person at the right place and time. A precise praise can stick in someone's heart and affect their direction for the better for years to come.

When I (David) was in fourth or fifth grade, I was not a popular kid. The conventionally awkward junior high years hit me early. I believed that wherever I went, whenever I opened my mouth, I annoyed people. I once overheard my teacher tell my mom that I would never attain higher education because I could not accomplish anything in her class. I felt that I had nothing to offer anyone. That estimation hung over me like a cloud and affected every interaction I had with people, even my family.

But my beliefs and behavior changed decisively because of my mom's best friend, Dianne Durrenberger. I thought Dianne was the coolest person in the world, and I learned that she saw me in a way that no one else did. One day she said to me, "David, people will want to be around you when they get to know you. You are funny and engaging to be around!"

Me? Funny? It was an incredible idea, but because Dianne said it, I believed it, and it changed me. When I would enter a room, I used to slink in sheepishly, slumped over. But after Dianne told me I was funny, I literally walked taller—my posture itself changed. When I entered a room with new people, I believed that as soon as they got to know me, they would want to hang out with me, and things would be fun. Like a self-fulfilling prophecy, that's what happened. I've never been the same since.

There are so many workers, especially younger workers, who never had a Dianne, but they are looking for one. Or perhaps they did have a Dianne in the past, but they still crave someone like that in the present. Many young workers do almost everything they do to win approval from someone. Some even go so far as to remove their social media posts if they do not get enough likes. Without trying to, many workers look at their supervisors as quasi-parental figures. They hope to gain from them either the affirmation that their parents never gave them or the affirmation that they counted on from their parents as children but are missing now.

We can analyze and pass judgment on this reality, but we ignore it at our peril. If people do not receive a steady drip of right-size positive feedback from their boss, they will look for a boss who *will* give it to them. If more supervisors understood and wielded the power of Precision Praising, fewer of their staff would quit.

Bringing Out Their Best

Hear us loud and clear: Precision Praising is not a crutch for emotional cripples. It is a rocket booster of confidence that brings the best out of talented people.

A couple of decades ago, I (Stan) orchestrated an album that I was producing. (That means I invented and wrote out the parts that a whole bunch of instruments would play on a song and at the same time determined who would play what notes and when.) We often brought a twenty- to twenty-four-member string section—musicians who played violin, viola, cello, and upright bass—into the studio to record while I conducted them.

After one recording "take," the head violinist followed me into the booth. "Stan," he said, "you really understand what a string section is supposed to do." Other times, after playing through one of my songs for the first time, the players tapped their music stands with their bows. (That is how string players applaud.)

The praise I received from these elite professional musicians boosted my confidence and poured fuel into my emotional tank. I was responsible for everything that was recorded, so the burden I felt was significant. I had been entrusted with a lot of money to get it right, but nobody knew whether what I had written would sound good until that recording session. So when I received praise from the string players at just the right moment, I thought, "Maybe I really can do this!" It didn't just give me confidence for that one project; it gave me confidence to attempt and succeed at much more for many years to come.

All of us are exposed to so much negativity from our environment, not to mention the doubts that arise within us. Negativity and doubts entangle people's beliefs about themselves, weigh

If people do not receive a steady drip of right-size positive feedback from their boss, they will look for a boss who *will* give it to them. If more supervisors understood and wielded the power of Precision Praising, fewer of their staff would quit. 🙌

them down, and make it easier for them to fail. Precision Praising is essential for human beings to perform to their full potential.

One time I (David) had a coaching session with a pastor who was really beaten down because he wasn't seeing the results he wanted. To make matters worse, he had just received the results of a personality type assessment he had taken. For the record, I see the value of those assessments, but depending on the circumstances, sometimes they can be truly depressing.

When this pastor read his results, he saw himself labeled with a type that he felt was fundamentally undesirable. "I'm a flake," he moaned. "I don't know why anyone would want me on their team."

I glanced over at the same chart he was looking at. I saw one sentence on the "shadow side" of his personality type and *a whole paragraph* on what is great about his personality. So I read that paragraph of praise to him slowly, looked him in the eye, and said, "I see all of this in you from spending time with you." I watched him drink in what I said, thirsting to believe that the way God made him was indeed good. That truth stuck in him and changed him. Later he wrote, "When I didn't like who I was wired to be, David showed me that I was worthwhile." That moment of Precision Praising changed his view of himself and helped him to be confident instead of despairing over the diminished person he thought he was.

The Sound of Silence

C. S. Lewis observed, "The world rings with praise—lovers praising their mistresses, readers their favourite poet, walkers praising the countryside, players praising their favourite game—praise of weather, wines, dishes, actors, motors, horses, colleges, countries, historical personages, children, flowers, mountains, rare stamps, rare beetles, even sometimes politicians or scholars. I had not noticed how the humblest, and at the same time most balanced and capacious, minds, praised most, while the cranks, misfits and malcontents praised least."[1]

We are sure that if you're taking time to read this book, you are not one of those "cranks, misfits, and malcontents." We are confident that you utter words of praise all the time. But even the most complimentary people can clam up at their place of employment. So what inhibits people—particularly leaders—from praising in the workplace and finding things worth praising in their coworkers?

1. **We're moving too fast.** When leaders attempt to encourage their people, they often toss off a light attaboy ("good job") amid the hustle and bustle. But it is hard to give someone meaningful praise while you are hurrying from one thing to the next—what you say hurriedly does not make much of an impact on the hearer.

2. **We're afraid of overpraising.** I (David) used to be afraid that if I gave people too much positive reinforcement, it would be meaningless—that eventually people would build up a tolerance to praise and ignore it. I thought if I withheld praise, then on the rare occasion when I did give a word of affirmation, it would be more powerful because I did not do it all the time. Yet I completely misunderstood that praise works best when it creates an atmosphere of continual affirmation (though, as we will see, the intensity can and should be varied).

3. **We do not enjoy people we do not know.** Lewis also believed that we praise what we enjoy because praise completes our enjoyment.[2] But you cannot enjoy what you do not know. Story Mining often comes before Precision Praising because you have to know someone well before you can praise them well, perhaps even before you *want* to praise them well. Without knowledge of your people, the praise you give them sounds generic and meaningless, not specific and meaningful.

4. **We train people to critique.** It is routine for worship teams, especially in large churches, to have a meeting after a worship service called a "debrief." A debrief is both painful and predictable. The leader asks, "What can we celebrate?" Someone volunteers, "God showed up." Then the leader asks, "What can we improve?" and the group starts picking things apart. It can be excruciating. Of course improvement is necessary, and in fact, every team with good people wants to improve without someone driving them to it. But people are so used to hearing "What could we do better?" that they lack confidence in what they have already done well.

5. **We don't need it (we think).** Many leaders don't give praise because they think they don't need it themselves. Maybe affirming words do not affect them as much as other kind gestures do, so speaking them to others does not come naturally. Or maybe they think strong leadership means having a "tough hide," and since they are tough, they treat others as if they are (or ought to be) tough too. (What is more likely true, however, is that

the leaders who have the hardest time giving praise are probably the ones who need it the most.)

6. **We're too proud.** You will not praise your team if you believe you don't really need them because you are talented enough to do the work yourself (maybe better than they can). And you will not praise your team for what they do if you believe you are deserving of their efforts.

7. **We're afraid of getting burned.** Subconsciously, many of us do not like the risk that comes with relying on people. So we inwardly try to hedge against the possibility that things might not work out: the person might leave us in the lurch, or we might have to fire them someday. Or we want to protect against being manipulated and taken advantage of. Yet to give real praise—to express that someone is valuable and we need them—is to get closer and more vulnerable than we might like. Therefore, many leaders keep their distance rather than risk getting hurt.

For any and all these reasons, the typical ministry organization does not, in Lewis's words, "ring with praise." When praise does leak out, it frequently falls just short of a compliment: "You did a good job, man." It is so vanilla that no one would ever remember it.

Is this the best that leaders can do? We don't believe so. We believe leaders can rise above giving praise that is as weak, ambiguous, vague, and cliché as a bulk-bought Christmas card with no signature. We believe that every leader can learn the art of Precision Praising and reap its great benefits.

Many leaders don't give praise because they think they don't need it themselves. 🙌

How Praise Changes Your Organization

As we illustrated previously, carefully crafted praise inspires people to perform to their potential. Yet praise can accomplish even more.

As we said earlier in the chapter, Precision Praising is "carefully crafting praise to inspire and course-correct your team." You read that last part right—*course-correct*. People usually think of praise as pure affirmation, something that reinforces what a person is already doing. This belief implies that praise and correction are separate tools in the leader's toolbox and are used for separate tasks, like a paintbrush and a wrench. But that is not so. For the skilled leader-coach who knows how to improv, praise and correction go together.

An Atmosphere of Praise

For starters, it is important to grasp a unique characteristic of Precision Praising. Unlike coaching competencies that are situational, occasional, or clustered at certain points in the relationship, **Precision Praising is continual.** A good coach uses it at the beginning of the relationship, at the end, and everywhere in between. The whole relationship is bathed in it. Like an IV drip, praise is to be delivered continually as a steady and nourishing flow. It is a recurring deposit made in the person's emotional bank day after day and week after week.

A person who receives genuine praise from their boss sees that relationship as positive and affirming. So when their boss has to deliver negative feedback—which is especially called for in a serious "you're about to drive off the cliff" situation—they have a balance in their emotional bank to cover the withdrawal from their self-confidence. They know their boss sees them as more than just the thing they messed up on.

But when negative feedback is not embedded in a consistently affirming relationship, the person often won't stick around to hear more. Harvard researcher Paul Green found that the more negative feedback an employee receives, the more likely they are to "shop for confirmation" of their worth by forging new networks and closing themselves off from the source of the negativity. In other words, they will seek out new coworkers and even a new boss to get the affirmation they crave. People who are struggling in their performance need correction to improve and survive, but they also need psychological validation. Green's research suggests that if a person has to choose between a correcting environment and a validating environment, they will choose validation every time.[3]

The solution is not to feed people correction in a "sandwich" (positive, negative, positive). People see right through that tactic; the praise appears ingenuine or insignificant, and its power is completely wasted. The only way to give people the correction they deeply need (and, in their hearts, want) is to make validation prevail in the atmosphere they breathe so that they feel secure when the moments of correction come.

Praise Redirects

An atmosphere of praise makes correction possible. But Precision Praising does more. Skillfully applied, your **praise can actually *be* the correction.** That's right: praise the right thing in the right way at the right time, and you can sometimes redirect a worker's behavior without issuing negative feedback.

One of the problems that arises from not being conscious

and intentional about our praising is that even when we praise well, we might be praising the wrong thing. People are so hungry for praise that, whether they admit it to themselves or not, they will do more of whatever they need to do to earn more praise. So unwise praising on our part can result in amplified behavior that isn't good for the person or for the organization.

For example, every business needs to sell its products and services, and some individuals in the organization are likely to be especially good at selling. But if you praise them for what good salespeople they are, do not be surprised if they become overly aggressive in selling. It is always important to appreciate people for their contribution to some degree. But if it is also important to your organization's values and brand not to come across to customers as a "sales culture," you must be restrained about praising the behaviors that will cause that culture to grow.

This lesson hit home to me (David) when my son Noah was in preschool. If there was ever such a thing as a "born leader," Noah is it. Even when he was a toddler, he had an astonishing charisma that seemed to get anyone around him, child or adult, to follow him and do what he wanted. Every time my wife and I would talk to his preschool teachers to find out how he was doing in class, the report was the same: "Noah is such a good leader."

But the teachers wouldn't stop there. They would also say, "But I would really like it if Noah would follow more, wouldn't interrupt, wouldn't divert attention from what I'm trying to do, wouldn't get upset when he isn't chosen as line leader," and so on. So we dutifully instructed Noah about the behaviors he needed to avoid or restrain. But our interventions never worked.

Then at one conference, I asked Noah's teacher a fateful question. "When you praise Noah, what do you praise him for?"

The teacher answered, "For being a good leader."

Bingo.

"How about we try a different approach," I said. "Noah doesn't need encouragement to be a good leader. I love that Noah's a good leader, but he's going to lead no matter what you tell him. The encouragement he needs is to be a good friend and a good listener."

So the teacher at school and we parents at home looked for moments when we caught Noah being a good friend or a good listener, and we praised him for it, using those exact words. Gradually Noah's behavior changed. Once we started praising him for the behaviors that would help him and his class, he made a decisive shift to a different behavior pattern without losing the strong leadership qualities that we still prize in him to this day.

Do you have someone on your team who is doing too much of one good thing and not enough of another? Think about what you praise the person for. Are you getting the results from the person that you have been encouraging all along?

Praise Shapes Culture

The potential of praise to change people for the better does not stop with the individual being praised, however. Next-level Precision Praising can change the culture of your entire team. **Your praise can shape your team when you praise one person in front of everyone else.** In such moments, you are not redirecting the person you're praising; you are redirecting the rest of the group. Precision Praising in public can do more for the many than it does for the one.

Jesus was a master at this. In fact, some of Jesus's moments of public praise were so powerful that they shaped not only his immediate team (the Twelve) but the entire Christian movement for two thousand years! Some of those moments of Precision Praising were recorded in the Gospels; we are the modern-day audience of those ancient points of praise as we look back in time through the Bible, and they continue to course-correct us today.

When Simon Peter declared his belief that Jesus was "the Messiah, the Son of the living God," Jesus singled him out in the presence of the Twelve. He called Peter "blessed" and named him the "rock" on which he would build his church (Matthew 16:16–18). Ever since, confession that Jesus is Messiah has been the square-one nonnegotiable criterion for being a Christ follower. What an impact that moment of praise had!

Interestingly, immediately after this episode, Jesus leveled Peter with an equally deliberate and public rebuke for trying to get him off track from his destiny to die and rise again. That rebuke firmly communicated to the Twelve that all of Jesus's followers would have to give up their lives just as he was about to do (Mark 8:31–38).

But that message did not stick right away; it needed repeating. So later, when a woman extravagantly poured her perfume over Jesus's head, he praised her to the disgruntled disciples by saying, "She has done a beautiful thing to me . . . to prepare for my burial." He did this to communicate again that he would not be around forever. He even predicted that the praise he gave her would continue to be remembered to correct his followers for generations to come (Mark 14:3–9).

Around the same time, Jesus saw a widow giving two almost

worthless coins to the temple. After Jesus got his disciples' attention, he praised her for putting more into the treasury than the wealthy who were ostentatiously giving lavish gifts, because she put in "all she had to live on" (Mark 12:41–44). Her name was not remembered, but the lesson was, and it shaped the culture of generosity and sacrifice in the early church (see, e.g., Acts 4:32–35).

These examples remind me (David) of a custom in my elementary school when I was a kid. It was called "Caught You Being Good." At the end of every school day, the teacher would point out someone she saw who was especially helpful and kind, and she awarded the student with a fake dollar to spend at the school store. When a classmate of mine got "caught" for picking up trash, did that ever make me want to pick up trash the next day! And I know I wasn't the only one. Those episodes of public Precision Praising made for quite a clean classroom. (Student ministers, take note!)

This lesson works not only with the *kids* in children's and student ministry—it works with the adult volunteers as well. When I was a student pastor, our church fed students every week. I had great volunteers whom everyone loved to be around, including the other volunteers. Even though I instructed my volunteers to mingle among the students and eat with them, every week I found the volunteers sitting down to eat together because they enjoyed each other so much. Whenever I reminded them to hang out with the kids, they would always apologize and do as I asked. But they would not do it on their own.

Then I changed to a new tactic: rather than remind the volunteers yet again to sit with the students, I called out one of the few who *did* do so, and I praised him in the presence of the other volunteers. Then—and only then—did things change, and when they changed, they changed big-time! Soon I stopped having to disperse the volunteers; they self-corrected to mingle among our students naturally and reliably.

Public praise is a powerful tool that **can inspire every team member to take responsibility** to make the team's meetings efficient and productive. You may have someone on your team who's always quick with a joke or a story that makes people laugh. People like being with this person, and you do too, but when their habit is indulged in a meeting, it sucks away the team's time and focus. (Think carefully: What is that person usually praised for? Is it for being funny? Hmm . . .)

What if you took time to praise the person on your team who exhibits great meeting etiquette? It could be as simple as recalling the last on-topic comment after the team gets off track. ("Emily, that was a great insight when you said . . .") Right away people will refocus because they unconsciously want to be the object of the leader's next praise.

There are other ways to use praise to shape meeting behavior—the possibilities are endless. I (Stan) once asked the worship staff at my church, "Who knows who's the most likely person on this staff to be on time?" After a moment of awkward silence, I answered my own question: "Timmy. Now, Timmy, tell us, where did you learn to be on time?" So Timmy started to tell a story from his childhood. As it turned out, in this small moment I combined Precision Praising and Story Mining, and both had a significant impact on this team.

Praise Unifies

One element of every healthy organization's culture is appreciation for each and every contributor. Taking care to appreciate each individual **strengthens unity** and enormously **boosts a team's effectiveness.**

After the New England Patriots won their sixth Super Bowl in 2019—they had appeared in half of the title games over the last eighteen seasons—respected columnist Sally Jenkins was asked how the team sustained such unprecedented dominance. While admitting that the complete answer is a mystery, Jenkins pointed out a rarely remarked characteristic of the team. "Success can sometimes really corrupt and ruin a team and their work ethic," Jenkins said. But the Patriots "never credit one player unduly to the point that it becomes a problem in the locker room. They have been almost religious on that subject. If you ask [head coach] Bill Belichick why he doesn't give [quarterback] Tom Brady more credit verbally, which has been an issue at times, he will tell you, 'There's 52 other guys on that team that I value just as much.'"[4] The important thing is that those fifty-two other guys *know* that their head coach equally values what they do because he says so in front of others.

I (Stan) have my own unique way of using praise to establish an appreciative culture in any room where I get to speak. I especially like doing it at the end of a daylong workshop or a grueling marathon of a meeting. I sign my name on a dollar bill. Then I get everyone's attention and announce that I want to celebrate and reward one person who made an outstanding contribution to what we did that day. I am careful to speak slowly and allow the drama to build. Finally, I name the person and ask them to draw near to get their dollar. Everyone applauds.

Sometimes I give my dollar to the most deserving person, but other times I give it to the person who I think needs it the most. Often I aim for the person who seems the most shy or the least confident. When I give a dollar to a person like that, I have seen them literally sit up straighter and walk boldly up to me afterward to thank me. Precision Praising is so powerful that it changes people's physical posture. That is because they know in that moment that someone values them.

In all cases, though, I deliver the praise in such a way that it **teaches a lesson to the rest of the team about valuing one another,** especially the people who tend to be overlooked.

I once coached a room full of big-shot human resources professionals gathered at a big-time church. At the end I did my dollar routine. Everyone thought I was about to honor somebody from some amazing church. (I secretly wondered how many of the participants believed I was about to honor *them.*) But I shocked them all when I gave the dollar to a volunteer sitting in the back whose role was to be our host, keeping us all comfortable and well fed that day. I announced, "The reason we're all in a good mood walking into this room is because of her."

I did not just praise that volunteer. I also taught those leaders the lesson about human resources that Paul taught in 1 Corinthians: "Those parts of the body that seem to be weaker are indispensable, and the parts that we think are less honorable we treat with special honor . . . so that there should be no division in the body, but that its parts should have equal concern for each other" (1 Corinthians 12:22–25).

Solomon wisely taught, "Do not withhold good from those to whom it is due, when it is in your power to act" (Proverbs 3:27). Recognizing the contributions of your people—*all* your people—is simply the right thing to do, and it **reinforces a standard of righteousness and fairness** within your team.

That inhibits the sort of infighting that wastes precious organizational energy, and it **propels teammates to pull together** in the same direction.

Nonpresent Praise

If public praise that shapes a culture is "next-level" praise, so to speak, then praising someone when he or she isn't around is next-*next*-level praise. It is a true art, and it has marvelous applications for building a strong team.

We once brought a new person onto our team, and at first it did not work out the way we had hoped. Market conditions were tough in his area of business, so much so that our team member thought we were probably going to eliminate his position or let him go. He was very discouraged. Monty (Slingshot Group's president) and I (Stan) were seriously praying about what to do.

While this was going on in the background, we had a company gathering where Will Mancini joined us. It was early in our relationship with him, and he did not yet know our team well. But as I drove him back to his hotel, Will told me privately, "I see a lot of potential in one of your guys," and he named the person whose job was at risk. Will had no idea that this team member was struggling.

By praising this member of our staff, Will redirected my thinking. Because he thought so highly of our team member, he caused me to see our guy through a different lens. This single conversation was a significant part of why we decided to keep him on board. And it paid off big-time: the guy is a rock star for us now, and we wouldn't want to go anywhere without him. Ultimately, the new perspective I gained from Will's praise accelerated our team member's progress by giving him enough time to come into his own.

When you get into the habit of praising others, you can praise people when they are not present to **create respect and appreciation** where they didn't exist before. You can create anticipation among existing team members for a new hire you are about to bring on board. You can **motivate people to work together** who are unsure of each other and are keeping their distance. You can give people with great potential the time they need to blossom. You can **smooth over accidents and misunderstandings** that cause tension among people. And every once in a while, when Precision Praising becomes a way of life, you can do all this without even knowing you are doing it.

The Art of Praising

As we have described, Precision Praising is an enormously valuable skill for a leader to develop. The key, of course, is not just *praising* but *Precision* Praising. Praise must be precise, and you cannot get precise without being intentional.

The first thing to focus on when you are trying to get precise is the person themselves. What is praiseworthy about this person? The easiest place to start is with whatever good thing they are doing in the project they are currently working on. But the real test of whether you are a good praise-giver is this: If all projects were put aside and the person wasn't doing anything for you, would you still have something you could praise them for? Praising is about seeing and enjoying the "otherness" in people. This is where Story Mining is invaluable. By learning someone's story, you enable yourself to see delightful things about a person that appear in all sorts of things they do, both at work and outside of work.

Knowing your team well helps you avoid casual, unconscious praising and instead use a high level of skill to give someone specific feedback. Unconscious praising hits the low-hanging fruit ("Nice job on that thing you did"). But Precision Praising goes deeper and makes a greater impact. It can **affirm who the person is at the identity level** and also who the person wants to become and could become if given the right encouragement.

Weight of Praise

I (David) had an experience as a pastor that you may relate to. After I preached a sermon, a woman came up to me and breathlessly told me, "That sermon was life-changing!" What an affirmation! I felt like a million bucks—by the grace of God I had said something that changed someone's life.

The next week the same woman came up to me again. "That sermon was life-changing!" she said. *Really? Two in a row?* I wondered. *That's cool.* But then the week after, she said to me yet again, "That sermon was life-changing!" At this point I started thinking along the lines of Inigo Montoya's remark in the movie *The Princess Bride*: "You keep using that word. I do not think it means what you think it means."

If you give an over-the-top praise too frequently, it loses its power; it becomes white noise. It can even seem disingenuous; it appears that either you do not know what you are talking about or else you are a flatterer. So part of Precision Praising is modulating the *weight* of praise. Different statements of praise have different weights based on the words you use (e.g., "life-changing") and how close your praise gets to the heart of a person.

Imagine a scale from one to ten. A praise weighted one is something nice but relatively superficial. ("I like those shoes.") A praise weighted five or six touches a standout contribution a person made. ("We have been so frantic this past month, but you've kept things moving so smoothly for us all; we couldn't have made it through without you.") A praise weighted ten touches a person deeply at the identity level; it affirms that the person truly is what they yearn to be. ("Do you know what a beautiful person you are? The kindness at the center of your soul is so pure and genuine and radiant that everyone who knows you sees it and loves you for it.")

Here's the important thing: a ten is *not* a superior praise to a one. They are both important. The key is choosing your spots—when to use one and when to use the other.

Once again, this requires knowing your people. Different people respond differently to the same praise. A six that is meaningful to one person comes across as a three to another. And it takes time to discover what touches a person at the deepest part of their soul.

Figure 2: The Weight of Praise Scale

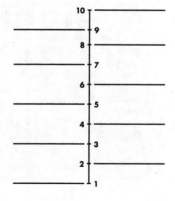

Weight of Praise Scale Case Study

As you learn what words of praise impact the people you lead, record what you discover on an actual Weight of Praise Scale for each person. This will refresh your mind to what affirms each member of your team, and it keeps your praise tailored to the individual.

The windup before the pitch is to listen before you praise—listen both to the person and to what other people praise the person for. You don't want your praise to become more white noise. Especially when you are searching for the right "heavy" praise, you want it to be creative and unique. If your praise stands out, the person won't soon forget it.

Timing of Praise

To be a good Precision Praiser, you need to know the person and you need to know the weight of your praise. But **you also need to know *when* to deliver it.** One time a guy I (David) coached said

Figure 3: One Person's Weight of Praise Scale

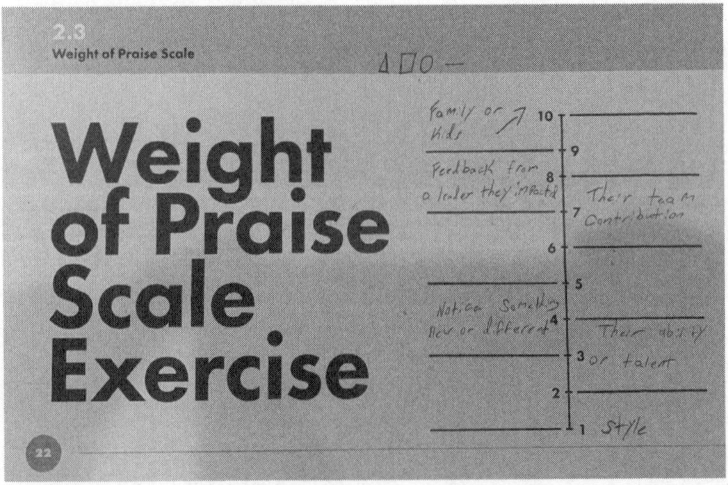

to me, "I said exactly what you told me to say, but it didn't work." When I dug a little deeper, I found that the situation when he delivered that praise was not right at all. Praise is like comedy: timing is everything.

Praise is also about pacing. When you praise, **you need to slow down as if you're driving in a school zone.** Precision Praising does not work when you or they are hurrying from one thing to the next. You have to slow down, get the person's full attention, and not rush your words if you want to make an impact.

One of the most important times to praise people is when the whole team is busiest and under the most stress. In those seasons, people sometimes feel such anxiety that they cannot clearly see that they actually love what they do and the people they do it with. They might instinctively look for the eject button. People really need encouragement at these times, and as their leader, you are to be the encourager-in-chief. Of course, during those periods *your* attention is liable to be most divided as well, so it takes intentionality to praise during those times.

Another especially important time to praise people is when they are not performing well. This is counterintuitive because it comes most naturally to praise someone when they do something great. But **when a person's accomplishments are least praiseworthy, that is when they need it most.**

We have a member of our team who once went for a long stretch without signing a contract. He got really down on himself. But our president, Monty, and I (Stan) just loved him and said, "We believe in you." We knew he was capable of more than the drought he was experiencing implied, and we told him so. Today he manages quite a lot of business. We helped instill

When you praise, you need to slow down as if you're driving in a school zone. 🙌

confidence in him when he was at his worst, and that got him through to the other side. "Strengthen the hands that are weak and the knees that are feeble, and make straight paths for your feet, so that *the limb* which is lame may not be put out of joint, but rather be healed" (Hebrews 12:12–13 NASB).

Finally, praise has a big impact on people when you **give it twice**: right when they do something good and again sometime later. Do you know how it feels when someone remembers something important to you and mentions it out of the blue? It makes you feel pretty special, doesn't it? The same happens when you say to a member of your team, "I want to thank you again for what you did a couple of months ago." Reiterated praise strongly communicates to that person that they are known and valued and that their work makes a difference.

Praise Drills

Achieving precision in praising is like dialing in the sight of a rifle—multiple shots are required to get it right. It is like adjusting the levels of a sound board little by little as a band rehearses. Precision is not an end state. It is a target you continually move toward over time.

So precision does not come all at once; it takes practice. When we hear a biblical scholar who is precise in their exposition of a particular Scripture passage, we know it came from practice. When we hear a pianist who is precise in their playing, we know it came from practice. And when we hear a coach who is precise in their praising, we know that came from practice too. So here are three specific ways you can practice Precision Praising today.

1. **Reverse engineering.** Think about a time when someone praised you such that it changed the course of your story (as in the examples we shared at the beginning of this chapter). With the help of the tool below, think about what was going on that made that moment of praise impactive, and look for clues for how you can create a similar moment for the people on your team.

Praise Reverse Engineering

1. What precisely were you praised for? What were the details and specifics of the praise?

2. How well did the person know you at the time? What was the scope and depth of your relationship with the person who praised you?

3. Was there something unique about the timing of the praise? If so, what?

4. Was there something special about the context or location of the praise? If so, what?

5. Did anyone else hear the praise? If so, how did the presence of others influence the dynamics of the praise?

6. What was the immediate impact of the praise in your life?

7. How often have you remembered that moment in your life? What has been the long-term impact?

8. Do you think the person would be surprised that you are talking about their praise now? Why or why not?

2. **Practice with your kids.** When my (Stan's) children were little, we had a saying stuck on our refrigerator: "If you want your kids to improve, let them hear the good things you say about them in front of others." Your children and grand-children need your praise so they can grow. There is no better group of people to start practicing praise with, and there is no better time than now.

3. **The "Seven Days of Praise" challenge.** For the next seven days, find opportunities to praise the people in your world (family, friends, coworkers, even a stranger). Take note of what this exercise does in you, as well as what it does in them. True, if you are not used to praising, people might start to wonder what is up with you. But if you use those seven days as an on-ramp to a life of Precision Praising, they will believe you are genuine, and they will appreciate you for it.

Precision Praising may not come naturally to you, but getting good at it is worth it. It guides people and helps them progress. It also makes you more attractive to everyone around you. People are drawn to a person who thinks more of others than themselves; they want to have that person around. Praising makes you the sort of person who gets invited to the party.

But one of the best things about practicing Precision Praising is that there are rarely negative consequences for not getting it quite right. What is the worst that could happen? What could ever be bad about looking at a beautiful sunset and remarking on it? That is what you're doing when you praise: you are remarking on the beauty in a person's life.

"So speak encouraging words to one another. Build up hope so you'll all be together in this, no one left out, no one left behind" (1 Thessalonians 5:11, MSG).

CHAPTER 5

Metaphor Cementing

Building a Bridge to Get
Your Point Across

When I (Stan) get on a plane, I often strike up a conversation with the passenger beside me. On one flight I discovered that the gentleman sitting next to me was an eye surgeon.

I had a question I was dying to ask him, but I kept my cool and let our talk play out until the right moment. (As we have said already, timing is everything.)

Eventually I asked my new friend, "Have you ever done surgery on somebody who is blind, and after surgery their family is sitting around them on the bed, and you unwrap the bandage and take the cotton off their eyes, and they squint, and they see for the first time?"

He smiled knowingly. "Many times," he replied.

Every leader encounters moments when members of their team seem blind. They are not unintelligent or stubborn; they simply cannot see what you can see about a situation. Leadership requires you to perform surgery to open their eyes to view their surroundings in a new way that fills them with energy for the work at hand.

To remove the injuries and blindness that block people's vision, leaders need the third competency of IMPROVleadership, *Metaphor Cementing*. Metaphor Cementing involves *using concrete illustrations to teach a new point of view that reshapes a person's perspective.*

The word *metaphor* comes from Greek roots, meaning "carry over" or "transfer." A metaphor is an image described by words. It helps people understand what they do not know well by comparing it to something they do know well. It uses humans' built-in talent for visual imagination and logic to carry meaning over from the known to the unknown.

Metaphor is baked into human language and perhaps even human consciousness. **We think in pictures.** Take an ordinary, seemingly literal sentence such as "It moved out of sight." Built into that sentence is a picture of vision as a *container*—vision "holds" something that may fall "out." All our thinking works like this. Neuroscientists have even used MRI machines to learn that when we hear imagistic language, it lights up different parts of our brains depending on how the image relates to the human body.[1]

Since this is how human cognition works, the leader who uses that reality to their advantage in an intentional way will have great influence on the people they lead. Leonard Sweet writes, "When someone is in the position to choose metaphors, that someone is in a position to mess with your mind, to change your perspectives, to generate new dreams."[2]

Jesus was a master of metaphor, and he used them in his leadership. As the greatest leader in history, he constantly taught his disciples about how to lead in the movement he was starting. Yet some of the most common vocabulary for leadership in Jesus's day was absent from his lips.[3] How, then, was Jesus to teach his disciples about leadership without using common leadership terms? He did it with metaphors: the steward, the slave entrusted with money to invest, the fisherman, the shepherd, the agricultural laborer, the brother, the friend of the groom. Jesus's metaphors for leadership enabled his followers to learn to lead the way he wanted them to, which they never would have grasped if he had used standard leadership language.[4]

I Have a Dream

When we (Stan and David) teach leaders about Metaphor Cementing, we usually begin with a legendary example: Dr. Martin Luther King Jr.'s "I Have a Dream" speech.[5] In many ways this masterwork is familiar, but listening to it again while hunting for metaphors in it—the whole speech, not just the most familiar part—brings an unfamiliar dimension of the speech to light.

Dr. King's speech is shot through with one metaphor after another. Metaphors appear in the opening sentences and never let up. We've italicized them below.

One sentence in, King intones, "Five score years ago, a great American, in whose symbolic *shadow* we stand today, signed the Emancipation Proclamation." At that moment, of course, Abraham Lincoln sat sculpted in marble behind him. This is the Abraham Lincoln whose Gettysburg Address—the only

American speech to rival King's in familiarity and power—begins, "*Four* score and seven years ago."

King says that "we" black Americans are "sitting in the shadow" of Lincoln. You may recall that King and his audience were actually standing in the sun at that demonstration. Yet the metaphor of "the shadow of Lincoln" not only hearkens to the epic significance of Lincoln's proclamation for black Americans that cast a long shadow into the future but is also a metaphor for the shadowy darkness of their plight in the hundred years after 1863.

King continues that Lincoln's proclamation "came as a great *beacon light*" to those "who had been *seared in the flames* of withering injustice." It was the "joyous *daybreak* to end the *long night* of their captivity." Since then, however, black Americans have been "*crippled* by the *manacles* of segregation and the *chains* of discrimination." They live "on a *lonely island* of poverty in the midst of a *vast ocean* of material prosperity." They are still stuck "in the *corners* of American society" as "an *exile*" in their own land.

As you note these metaphors piling up, keep in mind that we are only eight sentences into the speech.

Then King moves to a metaphor that he spends more time teasing out: the image of a *bad check*. America, he says, wrote in the Constitution and the Declaration of Independence "a promissory note to which every American was to fall heir," a guarantee of life, liberty, and the pursuit of happiness. Yet the country has "defaulted" on its promise: "Instead of honoring this sacred obligation, America has given the Negro people a bad check, a check which has come back marked 'insufficient funds.'"

Consider the power of that metaphor. Everyone standing in the August sun that day knew what it was like to receive a bad check. Everyone watching their televisions at home knew what it was like as well. It was a universal experience of adulthood for blacks and whites, men and women, rich and poor, old and young. Everyone could feel the anger at being the victim of disappointment, of a faithless promise. To reframe America's founding documents as a bad check was a succinct, radical, and unmistakable articulation of the view that civil rights activists had of America's fundamental problem.

Remember that at this point, King was still far from the more famous part of the speech that pronounces, "I have a *dream*." In fact, that section was not supposed to be in the speech at all. King scholar Marcus "Goodie" Goodloe says that when King worked on his address, his colleagues advised him not to use the phrase because he had done so several times in other speeches in the preceding weeks. Yet midway through King's prepared remarks, singer Mahalia Jackson, sitting on the dais, called out, "Tell them about the dream, Martin!" King obliged and did not look at his notes again for the rest of the speech.[6]

Think about how indelibly King's dream metaphor had stamped Mahalia Jackson. She was so captured by it that in that moment on the steps of the Lincoln Memorial, she had to hear again something King had said weeks before. Imagine speaking something to people in a way that is so powerful that they not only can't forget it but clamor to be told again!

This brief catalog only scratches the surface of the masterful use of metaphor in Dr. King's speech. Rather than go deeper, let us move on to a thought experiment.

Imagine that Martin Luther King Jr. had simply said in

Washington, "Things are not right, we have been lied to, and this needs to change." He would have been correct, and he would have been justified, but we would not be talking about it today. It would not be discussed in every school and written about by doctoral students. His remarks would have faded into oblivion. It is because King cast his message in the visual language of metaphor that it captures us and does not let us go.

The greatest communicators use metaphor as a painter uses a brush. It is a tool of their trade that they never leave behind. If we as leaders want to touch our people with a message that they cannot misunderstand and cannot ignore, we must learn to use the tool too.

The Benefits of Metaphor

It is impossible to calculate the advantages of adding Metaphor Cementing to a leader's toolbox, but we will try. Here are five of the greatest benefits of using metaphors in leadership. To paint the picture for you, we describe each benefit of Metaphor Cementing in terms of a metaphor.

Benefit #1: A Metaphor Is a Direct Flight to a Foreign Country

If you have a friend who is a native of another country, you have probably had conversations with them about what their home country is like. You may have strained to grasp what your friend describes to you; maybe you even viewed pictures of that unfamiliar place. Yet your comprehension of what that land is like remains fuzzy.

But imagine that your friend puts a plane ticket in your

The greatest communicators use metaphor as a painter uses a brush. 💡

hand and says, "I'm going back home for a visit, and you're coming with me." Hours after departing, you touch down in your friend's country and immediately comprehend what you could not comprehend before. It is not until you see that land in person, move around in it, even smell it that you finally understand what your friend had told you about.

Like that international flight, a metaphor is a link between what is known and what is unknown. It makes new connections between realities and our vague ideas about them. A metaphor **banishes blurriness.** It bridges the gap between your understanding and that of the other person. Like a Boeing 747, it launches a person's understanding to where it needs to go much faster than it could get there otherwise.

But metaphor goes beyond giving people new information. It also gives them new appreciation for the information they already have. With a metaphor in mind, people see the importance of something they did not appreciate before. Appreciation is crucial because without it, people do not move from understanding a principle to acting on it. To inspire your team to take the action that is critical to your organization, they must grasp not only the *what* but the *so what.* The right metaphor delivers it.

As our colleague Will Mancini puts it, IMPROVleadership is about getting to the heart of the matter and the heart of the person. Metaphor Cementing does that as quickly as possible; it shortens both distance and time.

Benefit #2: A Metaphor Is a Secret Ingredient

Everyone likes to eat tasty food. Yet there is nothing quite like taking a bite of something much tastier than you anticipated.

Very often when we eat, our attention is on something else,

such as the people with whom we are eating or something we are reading. But once in a while, a food has a flavor, a seasoning, or a spice that catches us off guard. Our eyes widen, our attention is disrupted, and we blurt out, "This is delicious! What's *in* this?"

Like a secret ingredient, a metaphor **grabs your people's attention**, which might be the most precious and elusive resource you have to manage. At the meetings you lead, if you do not draw people in, you miss the chance to cement them in a common goal. If you do not capture their imagination, they leave uncommitted.

Metaphor spices up the staples of organizational discussion that too easily become bland and tasteless, lulling people into passivity. Metaphor introduces people to new ideas and creates new synapses in the brain. It helps people love their work because they enjoy learning. Metaphor keeps us hovering above the mental routine. It turns any moment into a cognitive playground that is fascinating to explore.

Benefit #3: A Metaphor Is Allergy Medicine

Sometimes an idea can be so polarizing, uncomfortable, or threatening to people at an unconscious level that they will do anything to avoid it or even actively resist it. No matter what you say or how you try to word it, their defenses go up and they try to change the subject.

But delivering the same information with a well-chosen metaphor quiets the person's allergic reaction to that information. It **creates enough calm for them to be able to consider an unsettling idea** and receive it for what it is, not for what they fear it is. It fences negative emotion away from the conversation.

I (David) will never forget the first time I met Stan. Slingshot Group had recently hired me as a coach, and I was invited to a meeting of division leads. The meeting did not proceed very far before the discussion became intense.

Around this time, Stan walked into the room and quietly took his seat. In the middle of one team member's passionate speech, Stan leaned back, folded his arms, and suddenly interrupted. "Any of you ever been in the cockpit of an airplane?" he asked.

The room went silent. My immediate, inward reaction was, *Who is this guy, and what is he doing? We're about to get to an answer—why is he derailing the conversation?*

Meanwhile, Stan walked us through the instruments in an airplane cockpit and how to figure out the heading on which to fly. When he concluded his airplane metaphor, it had completely solved the debate we were in the middle of. The issue was solved, and no more discussion was necessary.

Stan's tactic did not make sense to me at the time—I did not understand what he was accomplishing until he had accomplished it. But later I realized that the power of Stan's compelling metaphor lay not only in its bearing on the issue at hand but also in its tie to his own life.

Whenever Stan uses an airplane metaphor, he is sharing something that is deeply personal to him. It is not a third-person story; it is a first-person story. So the metaphor goes beyond the propositional level of the conflict to the personal level. It reveals Stan's humanity and touches the humanity of the other people in the room. That is how a metaphor can "steal past those watchful dragons" of people's sensitivities to deliver truth behind their defenses.[7]

Benefit #4: A Metaphor Is a Backstage Pass

Sometimes a meeting or a dialogue with a high-level leader can be intimidating. If you ever feel you are not qualified to participate in certain conversations, you are not alone.

In those situations, however, metaphor can be a useful tool to gain an advantage in a situation where you might be at a natural disadvantage. If you have ten trusty metaphors in your tool belt, you automatically have something to bring to the conversation that you would not have had otherwise. Like a backstage pass, **a metaphor is your access to the ears, mind, and heart of an influential person.**

Recently I (Stan) talked with a coaching client who is a highly capable lead pastor. He is a fine communicator, but he speaks much too fast when he preaches.

One Monday over lunch, he asked me to tell him one thing I noticed about his message the day before. In that moment, I could have said, "You talked too fast," but he may have shrugged it off.

Instead, I said, "Well, you could be pulled over for speeding. You speak about ninety miles an hour." The startling humor in this image caused the pastor's wife to blurt out, "Thank you for saying that! We've been telling him this."

Seizing the opportunity afforded by the wife's comment, I went on, "What if you got someone to transcribe your message for four weeks in a row? You could read the transcripts word for word and eliminate the sentences that are not important. That will show you how you can still get your message across in the same time using fewer words, talking slower."

At the end of our lunch, the pastor and his wife told me, "Whatever we're paying you was worth it for that."

I've learned that high-level leaders are prone to ask questions that they already know the answer to. It is like a tennis serve: if I return it the way the person expects, they will smash the ball down my throat. But replying with a metaphor puts a wicked spin on my return: it forces the person to adjust and approach it more carefully than they would otherwise.

Metaphor not only allows your message to get through but also makes you a more distinguished communicator in the eyes of others, lending your words more persuasive force.

Benefit #5: A Metaphor Is the Page That a Book Falls Open To

Think of a well-worn book that you have read many times, especially one with a page you have gone back to repeatedly. The binding of the book is broken, and the spine is creased so that the book naturally falls open to the same place every time you drop the book or open it up.

Likewise, an apt and compelling metaphor is the point your memory keeps returning to every time you think of the concept it illustrates. Once the metaphor is rooted in the mind, you cannot think of the concept without thinking of the metaphor.

A metaphor may even serve as the memory's handle for a whole conversation. When a person remembers a metaphor spoken in a discussion, they are likely to remember the contextual dialogue that came before and after it. Metaphor Cementing is crucial for coaching because it **helps the person remember the instruction** their coach gave them.

I (David) was coaching a student pastor on the importance of being deliberate and strategic about where he places his effort to reach the students he wants to reach. At the time, we were walking along the shore of a large lake near his home. To illustrate my point, I picked up a stone and dropped it into the calm water. "If I drop the stone near the shore, the ripples don't go very far," I said, "but if I drop the stone farther from the shore, the ripples go much farther too. Where do you need to drop the stone in your ministry to have the widest impact?"

This metaphor cemented in the pastor's mind so firmly that he went back to his church and called a two-day retreat for his team to discern where to focus their efforts. He entitled the retreat Where to Drop the Stone. Because I used a meaningful metaphor, my coaching not only shaped his outlook but also changed the perspective of people I have never met.

Guardrails

Becoming a master of Metaphor Cementing takes practice and intentionality. As you think through the metaphors you are going to use in your next meeting, presentation, or one-on-one with a team member, here are three guardrails to stay inside of to make the most of those opportunities.

Stand on Common Ground

A metaphor works where your purpose and your audience intersect. The message you are trying to communicate must link up with the experience base of the people with whom you are communicating. In short, **use a metaphor that both you and your audience understand**.

A metaphor from surfing that I (David) like to use when I coach is wavespotting. When you are in the water with your board, waves come toward you one after another. It is not your job to generate them or to control them; it is your job to select the right one and let the others pass you by. The best surfers in the world choose the best waves to ride.

I share this metaphor with people who struggle with anxiety over all the things they think they need to do. I counsel them that only those items of greatest importance deserve their focus—their job is to spot the right wave.

I do not share this metaphor with everyone, however. When I am coaching a leader like myself from Southern California, where many teenagers surf every day, the metaphor works. But the metaphor usually has limited effectiveness with a pastor from the Midwest. Always choose a metaphor that stands on common ground shared by you and your audience.

Line Up Your Shot

In any game that involves getting a small object into a small area—from golf to cornhole, from billiards to basketball—a rushed shot is not likely to go where you want. You have to line it up and be careful before you deliver.

Similarly, you do not want to rush your metaphors. Do not be sloppy: imprecise language can distract people's attention away from your metaphor and frustrate what you are trying to communicate. If you say, "It's like cooking a cake," then for a split second, half your audience will think, "That's '*baking* a cake.'" They may still catch your drift, but the magic of your metaphor is lost.

When you employ a metaphor, **make sure you have your words just right**. If you are not sure of the right way to word a particular metaphor, perhaps it is better to use a different one.

Don't Paint a Picture—Build a Gallery

Metaphors are powerful, and therefore they are also dangerous. An inaccurate metaphor—or even an accurate one blown out of proportion—can communicate a message you do not intend. For the most important concepts in your organization, it may be best to have a whole gallery of illustrations. We don't mean mashing together so many metaphors in one breath that the hearer is left confused (although in the hands of a master, even that technique is effective, as in Martin Luther King Jr.'s "I Have a Dream" speech). We mean **using a variety of metaphors over time so as to work the same concept from different angles.** Taken together, this group of metaphors can display the complexity and nuance of an idea in a way that a single metaphor may not be able to.

Jesus built an astounding gallery of images of the kingdom of God from the everyday experience of his hearers. As John Adair points out,

> Jesus sounds as if he were talking about an actual place, not some abstract ideal.... In seven parables, the kingdom of God is compared to a house, while in six others the focus is on a great festive feast that takes place in a house. The "kingdom" can be entered or not entered ... one can sit down in it; people can eat and drink in it.... A man may be not far from the "kingdom of God." ... It has a door or gate on which one can knock and which may be locked.... Thus it is like a house or walled city.... Men are said to take it by force ... which described attackers storming a city.[8]

This rich group of metaphors gives people many ways to

imagine the unimaginable, the coming kingdom of God. At the same time, these examples also highlight people's liability to distort metaphors in the absence of good leadership. In light of these images of the kingdom of God as a house, is it any wonder that many Christians today confuse the kingdom of God with their church's building? These believers have lost touch with other metaphors of the kingdom as a dragnet, a field of grain, a mustard plant, yeast in a lump of dough, and a treasure hidden in a field.

Modern Christians' misunderstandings of the kingdom are not Jesus's fault—the early church seemed to get it—yet such perceptions illustrate an important point. For your most critical messages, make sure there is enough of a diversity of metaphors to make it difficult for one metaphor to be distorted in a way you do not intend.

That said, do not let these guardrails inhibit you from experimenting with Metaphor Cementing in your leadership. **It is better to use a metaphor and miss than not try at all.**

It is better to use a metaphor and miss than not try at all.

Your Crock-Pot

Being prepared to use a metaphor in any situation is the goal. But to do so, one must have a deep well of metaphors and also the depth of understanding and discernment to use them at the proper time. So when you are getting started in using metaphors more intentionally as a leader, we suggest that you gradually add ingredients to your Metaphor Crock-Pot.

Your Metaphor Crock-Pot might be a small notebook, a spreadsheet, or a note on your phone. It is a place where you store the metaphors that you are thinking about using. Simply brainstorm good metaphors (start with ten or twenty), write them down, and leave them alone to cook for several days or weeks. Return to them once in a while to see whether they are ready for use. Make adjustments and tweaks; remove some and add others. After a metaphor has been sitting in your Crock-Pot for a while, you will know whether it is ready to be served to the people you lead and when to do so.

The Crock-Pot's value is that it works your mental muscles that generate metaphors so that doing so becomes more natural with time. It might seem difficult at first, but it becomes easier once you get started.

Have you ever gone looking for a particular model of car to buy? Once you decide you want a Jeep Cherokee, for example, then suddenly everywhere you look, you see Jeep Cherokees. You never saw them before, but now that you are looking for them, they show up all over the place. Metaphors work the same way. The possibilities are endless, but you don't see them when you are not searching for them. But once you go on the lookout for metaphors, you find them everywhere.

If you need inspiration, a good place to start hunting for metaphors is this chapter. Go back to the beginning and count all the metaphors we use, elaborate and simple, obvious and less obvious, starting with the title. We explain ideas with metaphors throughout this book, but we packed as many as we could into this chapter to make a point.

Metaphors are one of the most powerful tools a leader has to help their team succeed and enjoy doing it. Metaphors expand your people's capacity to view the world in new ways. In Will Mancini's words, "Metaphors turn hearing ears into seeing eyes."

CHAPTER 6

Lobbing Forward

Helping People See All They Can Be

(Stan) recently received an unexpected text message from an old friend. I had led the music ministry in a church for some years, and this fellow was a volunteer who participated with the worship team there. His out-of-the-blue text hearkened back to a conversation we had at a going-away party that was thrown for me when I stepped down from my role. He wrote,

> You hit the nail on the head. The day you resigned from our church years ago, you told me that one day I would realize what it means to be a worship leader. My wife and I were called into a worship leading role at a tiny church with six people on the worship team seven years ago. Today I sat in front of a worship team of 45 people to talk about the direction we're going as a growing church and as a ministry. The reality and the weight of where God has brought my wife and myself hit me hard today and I was humbled. Thank you

for your leadership early on as I tried to navigate where God wanted me to go.

I said this text was unexpected, but that is not entirely true. I *was* surprised to receive it that day; I hadn't spoken to the guy in years, and I never would have guessed he would write me to express his appreciation (though that wasn't out of character for him). What did *not* surprise me about the text message was what this old friend is doing today. Of course, I could not have predicted the exact details, but I knew what I was talking about when I told him that someday he would realize what it means to be a worship leader. I saw something in him that he could not yet see in himself, and I spoke it. My message to him that day stuck in his memory and altered the trajectory of his life. I knew it would, and that was why I told him.

One of the greatest joys of IMPROVleadership is doing for our teams what I did for my friend, a competency we call *Lobbing Forward*. Lobbing Forward is *creatively challenging your team to look beyond the day-to-day grind of their jobs and into the future.*

When a person is staring down between their own two feet, their vision fastened on the gritty details of the urgent present that they have to contend with, Lobbing Forward is like a ball tossed high in the air that pulls the person's gaze upward. It elevates vision by pausing the routine to tell them, "This is what I see in you."

When a person's eyes are trained on the past—what they have done, what they might have done, what they wish they had done—Lobbing Forward is like passing a ball not to where your teammate is but to the open space where they can go. It turns their head in the right direction, and their body follows.

Lobbing Forward and Other Competencies

Bishop Joseph Garlington, a pastor and friend of mine (Stan's), says that nothing comes into existence that is not spoken first. God modeled this in the first sentences in the Bible when he said, "Let there be . . ." and it was so. Likewise, a new reality in someone's life always begins with a conversation of some kind. When you lob forward with someone, a change will immediately begin in their life—a change in the mind. The person is going to have thoughts they have never thought before, and that change cannot be undone. As Oliver Wendell Holmes Sr. put it, "Every now and then a man's mind is stretched by a new idea or sensation, and never shrinks back to its former dimensions."[1]

Lobbing Forward is one of the few coaching competencies focused on direct influence—not only asking questions to get a person to generate their own new ideas but **speaking authoritatively about where the person might go.**

Lobbing Forward becomes easier to understand when we compare it with other competencies of IMPROVleadership. You could argue that my words to the worship leader at his old church were an example of Precision Praising because Stan carefully crafted praise to inspire him. But Precision Praising is both more consistent and subtler than Lobbing Forward. You can (and should) praise every day, but Lobbing Forward **comes at a rare and special moment.** Precision Praising changes a person's trajectory just enough, and they may not be aware that it is happening. But Lobbing Forward is an unforgettable reorientation. It is an explosion of dynamite that cannot be missed.

This is not to say that Lobbing Forward has to be cast in

the form of a declarative statement. You can lob forward with a question like "Have you ever thought about . . . ?" But a Lobbing Forward question is not the same as a Story Mining question. A Story Mining question seeks to know who a person is today. A Lobbing Forward question **seeks to forecast who a person might become tomorrow.** Story Mining expresses appreciation for a person. Lobbing Forward expresses confidence in—and aspirations for—a person.

When People Need Lobbing Forward

A few years ago, a commercial for an air freshener product asked the viewer, "Have you gone nose-blind?" Most viewers quickly understood that "nose-blind" is a cute name for what happens when we get so used to a bad smell that we don't notice it anymore. But when someone unaccustomed to the odor walks into the room, they notice it right away.

Chances are, someone on your team has gone nose-blind. They are so inundated with the day-to-day stink of their situation that they can no longer adequately name the problem, or they may no longer even recognize that anything is amiss at all. Their ministry did not start out this way, but they were so immersed in it that they no longer remember that the current mess has not always been the status quo. The abnormal has become normal to them because of prolonged exposure. To them, the universe has shrunk to the dimensions of their own little world, and they don't realize it. They cannot see outside themselves to recognize the absurdity they are putting up with. They don't recognize other options of what could be, and they may even lack the will to try them.

This is one reason that a coach from the outside can be so helpful to people who are stuck. I (David) coached a student pastor who was hanging on for dear life. During their midweek gatherings, he greeted everyone at the door, he worked the snack bar, he signed families in, he ran the game, he delivered the message, and he was the last person to leave. He told me he was exhausted, but **he couldn't clearly recognize the source of the problem because he was so accustomed to it.**

My job was to lob forward with him. I was not nose-blind to his situation, so I could say, "What if you shifted the target of your ministry from keeping a program running to equipping people for service? What would your ministry look like three years from now?" I was able to describe a thriving ministry that he could arrive at in the future if he made adjustments now, first and foremost in his own mind.

Your job as a leader is to **make your team dissatisfied with the status quo** by stretching their minds. (We love the question Jared Kirkwood of the Rooted Network asks his team:

Make your team dissatisfied with the status quo.

"What do you need to know that you currently don't?") You yourself have to see above the day-to-day so you can help your team do so. You have to make them uncomfortable with how things are in a way that feels good, that energizes them for change. You have to lob forward to a future such that, once they picture it, they cannot be content with the present again. Once their minds go outside the invisible walls of life as they know it, they can never go back.

Freedom from the Past

Lobbing Forward is valuable not only to help team members who are stuck in the present but also **to help those who are (or may become) stuck in the past**.

When I (Stan) was twelve years old, I was in a terrible car accident. Three people were killed and one was hospitalized. Amazingly, I was not badly hurt at all—only a few minor cuts. But it was a traumatic experience, and it would leave a mark on me one way or another.

My pastor came to my house to visit me, and he said something that day that I never forgot: "Your whole life you will ask, 'Why did God save me?'" My pastor's statement lobbed the experience in a different direction than it might have gone otherwise. Instead of being stuck in guilt or confusion, I was able to gaze forward with hope. God saved me because he had a destiny and a calling for me to serve him on this earth. I did not stay trapped in the moment because I was directed to look ahead.

As another example, we have a team member (we will call him Stephen) who spent five years away from social media because of an episode in his career before he came to Slingshot Group. Stephen was afraid that if he went public about what he is now doing with us, people from his past would come out of the woodwork and accuse him of being unworthy of his current role because he had messed up before.

We told Stephen, "In light of the stuff you're doing with us and the impact you have now, we think you could put up with the criticisms of a few people from your past for a while. But that season will pass because of where you're headed." Lobbing Forward gave Stephen permission to dream again for the first time in a long time. It was difficult for him to reassume a public persona, but now he is sharing his wisdom with the world. He became a different person, humble confidence restored, because Lobbing Forward did not let him stay where he was.

The Difference Lobbing Forward Makes

IMPROVleadership is the art of helping your team to love their work so that they thrive and succeed in your organization for the long haul. Lobbing Forward contributes to this objective by **inspiring your team**. When people hear an encouraging word about the future beyond where they can reach now, they lean toward it. Boredom dissolves and interest explodes. Curiosity rises, conversation multiplies, and community deepens.

Lobbing Forward also **demonstrates deep care** for your team. That you have given thought to the wonderful places they might go in life tells them that you see, know, and love them. It shows in a big way that you are interested in them, you believe in them, and you have confidence in them.

Lobbing Forward **changes the person who hears it**, and that change is ultimately more significant than whatever destiny you suggest they might reach someday. When you ask someone a question about their future that begins with "what if," their answer is not what matters but rather that they are experiencing someone believing in them in real time. The shift in their mind as a result of the question is what makes the difference.

Likewise, the value of Lobbing Forward is **more about the journey it ignites** in a person than whether the described destination is exactly right. Success in Lobbing Forward doesn't mean correctly predicting an outcome but rather stretching a person. When God told childless Abram to go outside and count the stars, promising him, "So shall your offspring be" (Genesis 15:5), the point was not the precise number of stars in the sky. The point was to blow Abram's mind with a jaw-dropping comparison.

Caz McCaslin was the outreach director for his church. Like many churches with a large building, Caz's had a gymnasium, and part of his job was to fill the gym with kids from the community. Caz got good at that and filled it multiple nights a week with youth sports leagues he organized. His programs were so popular that he had kids on a waiting list. So he went to a big donor in the church and told him that he thought the program could impact even more people with a second gym. The donor agreed and gave the money to build a second gymnasium.

Soon Caz filled two gyms with kids who were playing sports and hearing the gospel with their families. But the facility reached capacity again, and there were still more children to reach. Caz went back to the donor and asked for money to build a third gym, but to his surprise the donor lobbed forward with him. "Caz, you don't need one more gym," he said. "You need a *thousand* more gyms. Churches all over the country have gyms. What could you do to fill all of them?"[2]

This awesome and timely lob got Caz thinking in a new way. It ultimately led to the birth of Upward Sports, a ministry Caz founded to help churches across the country reach hundreds of thousands of children for Christ each year. And by the way, Caz has since filled well more than a thousand gyms.

But what if he had not? What if Caz had filled only five hundred gyms? Or what if he had found a way to reach many more kids for Christ in a way that had nothing to do with church gyms? Would that have made the donor's prophetic advice a failure? Of course not! Lobbing Forward does not ride on accomplishing the thing projected; it succeeds when it leads someone on from where they are today.

The Future Job

On Saturdays when I (Stan) was a boy, I would put on nice clothes and go to my dad's furniture store. I imitated the salespeople by greeting customers when they walked in. It was not unusual for a customer to tell me, "With the way you greet customers, you could take over this store someday." They might not have known it, but they were Lobbing Forward with me, creatively challenging me to look ahead to my future.

As we said, however, the value of their comments was not that they drove me to become a furniture store owner. It was that they got me thinking about my gifts for interacting with people and how God might have me use them in the future. Sometimes I felt pressure when a friend of my dad's lobbed forward in a way that felt like rigid fate with a comment like, "When are you going to take over your dad's store?" But my dad himself never made me feel that way. He was supportive of the direction I sensed I was supposed to follow: not selling furniture in Illinois but making music in California.

Sadly, many people are forcefully lobbed forward to the wrong thing by influential voices, and many people have had no one lob forward in their lives at all. As a result, many people spend a huge amount of time developing the wrong skills and managing talents with which they were never endowed. One of the most important ways to lob forward is to **help your people catch a vision for where their talent truly lies** and how their vocation might evolve as they grow in it. As the leader who spends the most time with your team members in their work life, you have a special role and opportunity to help them see all they can be.

I (David) first experienced this in my work life at Parkcrest Christian Church. When Mike Goldsworthy hired me, he told me, "You're going to be our youth pastor, but I see more in you than that. We want you to be on our leadership team to help us figure out where we're going as a church." This invitation was new and unexpected to me; I was used to being looked at as someone whose job was to make things happen and hit targets, not as someone whose opinion was sought out by senior leaders. Being wanted for my opinions energized me in a fresh way and got me to lean in to how my role could advance what the whole church was doing.

Later I came aboard at Slingshot Group. After Stan had established enough rapport with me that I felt secure in my position on the team, he told me, "I don't know what you're going to be doing in three years, but it's not what you're doing now." When I asked him what he meant, he simply replied, "I don't know," but his comment kickstarted my imagination. What might my future at Slingshot be?

Look There, Stay Here

The notion of imagining out loud with a subordinate about their career trajectory makes some supervisors uncomfortable. Their uneasiness might be rooted in a fear of giving false hope about internal opportunities that may not materialize.

But a larger fear may be the threat of *external* opportunities. In this book, we have claimed that IMPROVleadership saves organizations money and increases productivity because it helps them hold on to their best people. But a reader might wonder whether affirming a person's talents would whet their appetite for a new position somewhere else, especially if their talent lies beyond the boundaries of their current job. Lobbing Forward may look more like a risk than risk prevention.

In still other cases, a supervisor's hesitancy to lob forward about a team member's vocation may come from a darker place. Leaders may not lob forward with their team because they believe that the people on their team are already right where they belong. The leader has no vision that a person reporting to them could be more than they are. The leader may not even consider the idea except as a threat viewed through the lens of their own jealousy and insecurity. Many leaders feel insecure at the possibility that their people might not "know their place"—that is, below or behind the leader—and they want to keep them there. Sadly, many leaders assume this posture naturally because that is what their own supervisors have always done to them.

Ironically, however, efforts to keep people in their place or to discourage them from outside opportunities only increase the dissatisfaction and restlessness that spur people to look elsewhere. If you want to keep your best people, **the safest thing you can do is to imagine with them all they could do and become, even if it is not with you**.

If Stan had not told me that I would be doing something different in three years, I would have grown bored and would have kept my eye out for the next thing somewhere else. Part of the reason I am at Slingshot Group today is that I love working for an organization that believes I can do more. When Stan lobbed forward with me, I got the message he was trying to send: "I respect you so much that I don't care what you do with our company—I just don't want you to leave."

When you lob forward with someone about their vocational future, you are telling the person that you care more about them than about the job they do for you. Even if your lob directs their gaze beyond your organization, they know you want to help them move forward without moving them out, and that draws them back in.

Nevertheless, it is true that when you lob forward **you have to be careful not to be too specific about a future job in your own organization**. You don't want to make a promise you cannot deliver on. But despite the future orientation of Lobbing Forward, the main subject is a person's qualities in the present. Lobbing Forward says, "This is the good thing I see in you."

Indeed, Lobbing Forward to a possible future role **motivates solid people to give their best to their present role**. It helps people reimagine the job they are currently doing. It inspires a person to "clean their plate"—to master their current assignment—to prepare for their next course.

One of the simplest ways to inspire a person with a glimpse

of their potential without making lofty promises is also one of the best ways: ask their opinion. As Mike Goldsworthy did with me, invite the person into a conversation that is above their pay grade, and listen seriously to what they have to say. The ordinary words "What do you think?" have an extraordinary ability to elevate a person's confidence, energize them, and assure them that they matter to you and to your organization.

Preparing to Lob

As with other competencies of IMPROVleadership, committing to practice Lobbing Forward initiates a change in the leader before there is a change in the people being led.

Lobbing Forward **requires a leader to be humble**. It takes humility to believe you are in the presence of greatness when you speak to a person considered your subordinate. But unless you have that humble posture, the person will not hear you or believe you when you lob forward with them.

You also must **have sincere interest in the person**. They need to sense that you are genuinely fascinated by who they are, where they have come from, and where they are going. You must truly care about their past and believe in their future.

For this reason, if you want to lob forward with someone you spend a good deal of time with, **an established pattern of Precision Praising sets it up well**. As noted earlier in the chapter, Lobbing Forward overlaps somewhat with Precision Praising. Just as you vary the weight of your praises, you can (and should) vary the weight of your lobs. But even the lightest lob is as massive as a heavy praise. So if you are not in the habit of praising a member of your team and you suddenly lob forward with them, it will seem weird. Their head will be turned the wrong way, and they will not catch what you throw.

The person you are Lobbing Forward with needs to know you want to help and maybe even serve them, not manipulate them. Your projection of the future has to be a future that is truly good for them, regardless of whether it helps you; it cannot smell of an outcome that suits your interests but may not suit theirs. Lobbing Forward is to be a gift, not a contract.

You also have to **know your people well**, which is why Story Mining is so helpful. You want to lob forward to just beyond what they think they can reach even with a great deal of effort. A lob that falls too near is a mere exhortation, and one that goes too far sounds like nonsense. You also have to know what inspires the person and what their aspirations are. Saying, "You could be another so-and-so," comes across completely wrong if they have no desire to be like so-and-so at all.

The word *entice* comes to mind when I (Stan) am in the

Lobbing Forward is to be a gift, not a contract.

Lobbing Forward mindset. As a kid, I loved to fish with a rod and reel. I was pretty good at casting the bait in the right direction to land it at the most strategic place in the pond. If I landed the bait too far from the fish, it had no impact; the fish was not even aware the bait was there. If I landed the bait right on top of the fish, it would swim away startled. But if I landed the bait within sight of the fish and wiggled the pole just a little, the fish was enticed, and soon I held it in my hands.

Toss High

The actual delivery of a lob has much to do with finding the right moment. Again, unlike Precision Praising, Lobbing Forward does not happen every day, so the choice of words and the search for the right opportunity need to be bathed in prayer.

There can certainly be special moments to lob forward with someone in a public or group setting, but it is **more often done in private**. It requires carving a special one-on-one out of the day-to-day. That way the person knows they have your soul in that moment. Maybe even the volume of your voice should be quieter and more intimate—this is life-changing stuff.

Slowing down is built into the metaphor of Lobbing Forward itself. If you have ever played the yard game called "cornhole" or "bag toss," you know how important it is to take your time. To score in cornhole, you have to toss a beanbag from a distance so that it comes to rest on a sloped wooden board or falls through the hole in it. If you throw with a low arc, the beanbag travels fast to the board, but it skips off the surface without scoring a point. Instead, you have to throw with a high arc that gives the beanbag a long time to reach the board. When it drops steeply onto the board with a satisfying thud, it sticks there and scores.

The same is true with Lobbing Forward. When you rush it, it skips off the person's consciousness and does not stick in their memory. But when you slow down your speech, wind up patiently, and toss a high-arcing dream at the person, it hits with a thud. The conversation comes to a halt for a moment as the person digests what was said. If it is something they never would have thought on their own, they will not forget it.

As to how exactly you phrase the lob, **some tried-and-true word choices work well.** A great starter is "I wonder if . . ." Also work in what grammarians call modal verbs, such as *can* and *could*, *will* and *would*, *shall* and *should*, *may* and *might*, *must* and *have to.* It can be effective to use these in open-ended questions. Here are a few to get you started. Experiment to find your own style of Lobbing Forward.

LOBBING FORWARD QUESTION STARTERS

- Does it have to be this way?
- What would happen if you . . . ?
- Who says you can't . . . ?
- _____
- _____

Immeasurable Impact

It probably has not escaped your imagination that you can **lob forward with entire teams as well as with individuals.** When you do, the results can be amazing.

One of the best examples of this that I (David) have ever seen was at Transformation Church in Tulsa, Oklahoma, with lead pastor Michael Todd. I was invited to speak at the church's staff retreat. I arrived a bit early, so I sat in on their staff meeting. As I listened, Michael lobbed forward an audacious dream that he had been imagining for a few months. He projected a photo of Tulsa's SpiritBank Event Center, an arena and conference facility, with the church's name Photoshopped across the sign. Then Michael said, "I believe that this is the future home of Transformation Church. It doesn't make sense because it isn't even available now, and it's too big for us, but I see it being our home. When it comes available, we're going to buy it because I believe that in the next couple of years it will be where we do church."

When Michael made this announcement, I thought, "No way. This is not going to happen." But I was still moved in spite of myself. The lob energized me, and I was not even a part of the church!

After a while, Transformation Church did indeed buy the SpiritBank Event Center. They were doing plenty of renovations to prepare it for regular use, but in the meantime, they decided to have their upcoming annual conference in the center to give it a test drive. But during the conference itself, they changed their minds. Part way through the conference, the church took up an offering called "We Can't Go Back" to buy production equipment in order to stay in its new building permanently. Transformation Church has worshiped there ever since. Michael Todd's motto is "It's only crazy until it happens."

Lobbing Forward does not always have an impact that you can see splashed over a huge commercial building. Sometimes you don't see the impact at all because it manifests far in the future, beyond where you can see.

Once when I (Stan) was at a conference, someone recognized

me and approached me to introduce himself. "Stan, you don't know me," he began, "but you changed the entire trajectory of my parents' ministry."

The man's parents were traveling worship leaders, and at one of their stops many years before, they happened to meet me, and we had a conversation. I lobbed forward with them by giving them an idea of how valuable it would be to their ministry if they would make recordings and have them available when they gave a concert. They had never considered doing such a thing, but they took my advice, and it caused their ministry to blossom. The man concluded his story by saying, "I am a worship leader myself now, and I probably never would have become one if you hadn't given my parents that idea."

Lobbing Forward is that powerful. You may never know the impact you have by elevating people's vision above the gritty grind of ministry to see the horizon ahead.

CHAPTER 7

Going North

What Makes a Detour the Fastest Way Home

When I (Stan) was a boy, I used to go rabbit hunting. Imagine walking into a field of waist-high brown grasses or into the woods, looking for a quiet brown animal perfectly built to conceal itself. No matter how many times you crisscross that field or walk through the woods, the rabbit always seems to win.

So when I went rabbit hunting, I always preferred to go with a buddy who had a beagle. With its superior sense of smell, the beagle knew just where the rabbit was, so we would stand still and just watch while the beagle ran through the brush. With its tail wagging happily, it would soon pick up the scent of a rabbit and start whimpering. When the dog made contact and saw the rabbit, it barked loud enough to be heard a quarter mile away. It was the coolest sound.

When a rabbit senses danger, its instinct is to run directly away from it. But according to the beagle's ingenious training, it drove the rabbit *sideways* instead. For example, if I stood off the west edge of the field, the rabbit would naturally want to run east, but the dog pushed the rabbit to get away by going *north*. Making a noisy, barking racket all the way, the beagle then guided the rabbit to turn east . . . then south . . . then west, right back toward me. Eventually, with the dog hot on its heels, the rabbit would burst out of the field in my full view. The rabbit thought it was running straight away from the intruder, but by going north first and then turning in a gradual circle, it was lured right to me.

Leading your people as a coach requires you to employ the competencies of IMPROVleadership, and you may have noticed that the ones we have looked at so far are very people-affirming. But even in the most affirming work environment possible, leadership is not always a cooperative endeavor. Sometimes people resist doing what they need to do and moving where they need to go. You may have multiple one-on-ones to direct a team member to improve, yet no change follows. What do you do?

This is a common problem in coaching; in fact, it is a given. Legendary football coach Tom Landry is said to have defined coaching as "helping people do what they don't want to do so they become what they want to become." Most people do not change without someone to hold them accountable. Often what people most need for their own benefit—even when it is something they believe and say they want—is something they resist tooth and nail when push comes to shove.

When going at the issue directly does not work, you can get them to grow only by luring them back to you. Like an eagle with a broken wing whose every instinct is to avoid contact with humans, some people have flight instincts that force you to trap them in order to heal them.

This is what we call *Going North*: *using indirect influence to redirect a person's thinking or perspective*. Indirect action may be riskier than direct action because more variables are outside your control—you are taking a chance, hoping that things ultimately end up where you want them to go. But indirect influence may work when a direct approach goes nowhere.

Going North is about making moves a person doesn't expect that draw them where they need to be going, even when they don't realize it. It is zagging when they expect you to zig. Whether you go north to establish a relationship or to overcome an obstacle, the other person may not even realize you are doing it.

The Desk That Was More than a Desk

For me (Stan), an especially memorable example of Going North has to do with my daughter Sara. As a talented young woman, Sara was hired for a responsible position as a producer in a highly prestigious church in a city thousands of miles from where she grew up. It was quite a trying time for her. Not only did she have to contend with entrenched interests in her area of ministry, but she was also very lonely in her new city.

Sara called me weeping in the middle of one workday. She was at her limit and was profoundly sad. I was ready to jump on a plane immediately and go bring her home, but I stopped myself and asked her a question first. "Sara, where are you right now?"

"My office," she tearfully replied.

Sara shared an office with another staff member, so I asked a follow-up question. "Sara, who or what else is there in the office with you right now?"

"No one," Sara answered. "Nothing abnormal but a box with a new desk for my officemate."

Still going north, I told Sara to open the box and tell me what she saw. "Just parts of the desk, Dad, and a set of instructions."

"Okay, Sara," I said. "I want you to take everything out of the box and put the desk together. Follow the instructions. Then call me back when you're done."

Sara was puzzled, but she agreed. She had never assembled a desk before, but she applied herself to my assignment, and it started to come together. As Sara finished up, her officemate walked in. She was stunned that Sara had put her desk together for her.

My assignment for Sara accomplished several things. It distracted her from her agony for a few moments. It forced her to do something physical, which is beneficial for emotional well-being. It took her eyes off herself as she served somebody else. And it created a new bond between her and her officemate that reduced her loneliness a little.

The task of putting together a desk did not directly address any of the problems she had, but it indirectly touched all of them. That assignment proved to be a turning point in Sara's time at that church. She became willing to stay there a couple more years, and to this day she looks back gratefully on what she gained from her time there. It all started by going north when Sara felt she had nowhere to go.

Barriers to Someone's Best

Going North is useful **whenever a person consistently resists good ideas.** There may be any number of reasons they do so. They may fear change or its consequences. They may be afraid of being exposed as defective in some way. They may have absolute conviction about a course of action based on incomplete knowledge or experience. They may react to an idea as a violation of personal values that they have not named and that ride below the surface. Any of these reasons may be valid, invalid, or a mixture of both, but if they hold a person back from going where they need to go, these reasons need to be circumvented by a skilled leader.

The most formidable barriers may reside in the hearts of the most confident people. Frankly, the more accomplished a person is, the more likely they are to be full of themselves. Of course, they don't perceive this and would completely deny it if you confronted them directly. But their smug self-assurance erects a barrier that keeps them from learning what they do not know.

Part of a coach's job is to **help people see the truth** about their situation. Telling a person that they are ridiculous is ineffective because they will fight you on it. Instead, you have to **hold up a mirror so they can see it for themselves**.

I (Stan) have gone north on overconfident leaders by engaging in light conversation about what it means to be the best. I might ask, "Do you think there is someone in the world better than LeBron James and Michael Jordan who hasn't been discovered yet? Do you think there ever will be?" Or I might say, "You seem to be at the top of your game. Do other people in your life think that's the case?" I might even say, "I met a couple of your staff over lunch. Really quality people. You're probably too busy to have too many stories about them, but could you tell me one about them?" Any of these questions can get a self-assured leader to start running north.

The most formid-

able barriers

may reside in the

hearts of the most

confident people.

Going North is a game of slowing down speedy people and maneuvering around the barriers they erect to get to their hearts. It is a strategy game. Some might see it as manipulative, but we do not. Sometimes we are forced to outwit a client because they are actually opposing themselves, not us.

To go north with your team, **you have to be willing to slow down.** You have to set up situations and conversations that many leaders don't have the patience to get into. Most organizations are moving as fast as they can, and the fastest thing a leader can do is to issue a direct order. But there will always be times when going straight at a person or an issue will not accomplish anything but offending the person and making them even harder to move. The most direct route to the rabbit is to plunge directly into the middle of the field, but the most effective route is to go north and wait for the rabbit to come to you.

The Fundamentals of Going North

Going North is one competency that incorporates a host of tactics. There will always be more than one path around the barriers that people throw up. Here are the five fundamentals of Going North, with examples not only from our own experiences but also from the Master of Going North, Jesus.

Fundamental #1: Reveal Common Ground

The first way to go north, especially at the beginning of a relationship, is to find "uncommon common ground" with the person. We mean **a shared interest or experience that is startling and unexpected.**

Picture Jesus's encounter with the woman at the well

Going North is a game of slowing down speedy people and maneuvering around the barriers they erect to get to their hearts.

in John 4. He is a man; she is a woman. He is a Jew; she is a Samaritan. As would soon become evident, he is holy and law-abiding; she . . . isn't. Everything in their world says that they have nothing in common, and it would be a scandal for them even to greet each other.

Then Jesus breaks the silence with the words, "Give me a drink." Lo and behold, they have something in common after all: they are both thirsty. Jesus goes so far north that the woman has no idea where she is, but as the conversation proceeds, he leads her right to himself, the source of living water.

In our work with Slingshot Group, a supervisor often brings us in to coach one of their employees. From the get-go there is almost always a barrier to navigate. Understandably, the person is usually nursing many suspicious questions: *Why does my boss think I need you? Are you here to judge me? Am I going to lose my job? What do you know that I don't know?* The coach's job is to get around that barrier and draw the person into a constructive relationship.

One time I (David) was called into a church by a senior pastor to coach their youth pastor. After a wearying cross-country flight, I was introduced to a guy who was frosty from the start. It was apparent that he thought he was too good for this experience—and that if something did not change quickly, my six hours of travel would be for nothing.

As he led me to his office, I looked this way and that for some way to break the ice. I caught a glimpse of a ping-pong table in the youth room, and I took a shot. "Hey, do you play ping-pong?" I asked.

His eyes glittered. "Yeah, I do," he replied.

I knew it was on. "Me too. Want to play a game?" I asked.

After a competitive game of ping-pong, complete with light trash-talking, we resumed our walk through the church. We found our uncommon common ground, and it changed the mood decisively. We both loosened up. It was the beginning of a successful and productive coaching relationship.

Fundamental #2: Surprise with a Gift

Giving an unexpected gift—or giving a gift in an unexpected way—opens doors in a relationship and spins it in a new direction. It kindles goodwill or serves as an unexpected object lesson.

Think of the unforgettable moment when Jesus went north on Simon Peter by giving him fishing instructions (Luke 5:1–11). Simon was already a disciple of Jesus like dozens of others, splitting time between being instructed by his rabbi and carrying on his daily responsibilities as a businessman and family man. But Jesus was about to call him to follow at another level.

Simon had had a terrible night fishing, catching nothing. After cleaning up, he waited patiently to go home while Jesus used his boat as a pulpit. But after Jesus dismissed the crowd, he told Simon to go out again and try for a catch one more time. The result was so many fish that the catch started tearing the net and required two boats to bring it ashore.

Jesus's astonishing gift of fish was a jackpot for Simon and his partners. But it compelled Simon to look at both himself and Jesus in a shocking new way: "Go away from me, Lord; I am a sinful man!" he cried (v. 8).

But Jesus had other plans: "Don't be afraid; from now on you will fish for people" (v. 10). Simon Peter and his partners left their businesses for good to follow Jesus.

A surprising gift can especially help get things going at the beginning of a relationship. I (Stan) once saw a video of National Geographic photographer and keynote speaker Dewitt Jones and was completely enamored of his pictures. I reached out to him, and he graciously invited me to spend time with him before he gave a talk to a group of executives.

To establish rapport with Dewitt, I felt that I had to give him a gift; after puzzling over it, I finally settled on one. When we met, Dewitt opened the professionally wrapped package (thanks to my daughter, who worked at Nordstrom's), and to his surprise, he found a yellow, cardboard disposable camera. "Can you take a good picture with that?" I asked.

He grinned broadly. "I sure can," he said. It led to a delightful conversation and an ongoing relationship.

A gift can also establish camaraderie on a team. When I (David) took over leadership of Slingshot's coaching division from Stan, the transition was smooth. Having been part of the team for several years, I was a known figure, and little changed in the coaches' day-to-day lives. But to establish a new kind of rapport with the team, I ordered enamel pins with the Slingshot Group logo and gave them to each team member with a handwritten note. It was a way of creating a fresh feeling of solidarity for our division and a way of expressing my appreciation to each member individually.

Fundamental #3: Disrupt the Setting

Another path north is to disrupt the setting that the person is used to functioning in. We don't mean messing up their desk; we mean **taking them out of their element to have a conversation in a different space** where they can gain a different perspective.

Jesus repeatedly disrupted the setting with his disciples by traveling with them. He took them across the stormy Sea of Galilee to show them his power over the natural realm and landed near Gadara to show them his power over the spiritual realm (Matthew 8:23–34). He took them out of Jewish territory to the pagan city of Caesarea Philippi to have a conversation about his true identity, and he took three of them to the top of a mountain to display that identity before their eyes (Matthew 16:13–17:8).

When we meet a new coaching client, we always do some variation of what David did when he played ping-pong—we have our first conversation out of their office, even if it is just going out to lunch. A different setting stimulates casual banter that often can be more revealing and important than professional Q and A.

I (David) learned in one job how worthwhile it was to go north on the lead pastor by disrupting the setting. When I started in that role, another person on staff advised me, "When you need to get through to the boss, ask him to go to the batting cages with you. He will say yes any time of day." Sure enough, when I saw that he was blocked or overwhelmed, I would invite him to hit baseballs. After he hit a few line drives, I could ask him about what was going on, and we would have a far more productive conversation than we would have had in the office.

You can disrupt the setting even more dramatically, especially when there is a lesson you want to help someone learn. Once when my (Stan's) son went through a difficult time in high school, I had a lesson for him that I hoped would help him overcome the trial he was in, but it was hard for him to hear it. So I took him to visit a friend of mine who was dying of cancer.

My son and I both had to crawl into full protective gear before we were allowed to enter the room so we would not introduce disease that his weakened immune system could not fight off. It was an unforgettable experience. After the visit, my son was ready for a real talk with me.

Speaking of teaching a lesson, a great technique for disrupting the setting is swapping the roles of teacher and student. When I (David) was a kid, my uncle wanted to teach me to box. He piqued my interest by asking for my advice. He would describe a hostile situation and ask, "What would you do?" I realized pretty quickly that I had no idea how to answer his questions. It made me much more interested in learning how to defend myself, and I started heeding my uncle's advice. Reversing roles is a display of humility that cultivates interest and openness to learn when the person you are coaching has put up a wall.

Fundamental #4: Teach Using Story

A story often can do what other words cannot. A listener may be defensive, uninterested, or even bored when they hear direct advice. But the same person may be drawn in by a story because they become emotionally invested in how the problem posed by the plot will be resolved. The listener can then reflect and draw personal conclusions. **A story puts the opportunity for change in the hands of the listener**; if they take the bait, the change they experience is personal and permanent.

A number of Jesus's parables are stories, perhaps the richest example being the one known as the parable of the prodigal son in Luke 15. The occasion for this parable's telling is the Pharisees' open criticism of Jesus for welcoming "sinners" and eating with them. Jesus replies with a couple of illustrations that explain and defend his actions: his mission to bring sinners to repentance is like a shepherd looking for a lost sheep and a woman looking for a lost coin. But these analogies only parry the Pharisees' blow; they are unlikely to win them over.

So Jesus tells a story about a man with two sons, filled with drama, pathos, and surprise. The outrageously dishonoring younger son is portrayed to stoke the Pharisees' hopes that he will get what is coming to him. But his repentance among the pigs also might elicit sympathy from the Pharisees in spite of themselves, especially when the son intends to do the "right" thing by admitting his failure and accepting the punishment of being disowned by his father.

The Pharisees had to be hanging on Jesus's every word. What *should* happen to the son? What was the father going to do when the son got home? How would this story end?

Jesus shocked them by depicting a father who falls over himself to welcome the son back home. But before they can fully absorb this bewildering plot twist, they learn that the story is not over, because attention now shifts to the older son. A new problem emerges: by being publicly unwilling to join the younger son's homecoming party, the older son has dishonored the father too. How will this tension be resolved?

We do not know. Jesus tells how the father mercifully and meekly appeals to his son to join the celebration, then stops speaking and stares at the Pharisees. (The silence must have been unbearable.) His point was clear: *You tell me, Pharisees: How does this story end? Will the older son—the character who represents you—join the party?* They had no answer. Jesus used a story to go way north on the self-assured Pharisees and led them right where they did not want to go.

When I (David) worked with our student ministry search division, I would sit down with a client and have a blue-sky session to hear what they were looking for in a candidate. It was not uncommon to learn that they wanted a unicorn, something that does not exist: "We want a student pastor who is prestigious but also gregarious, someone who could be a scientist if they wanted to, or a fashion model." The longer the list grew, the more ridiculous it became.

I would listen patiently and take notes dutifully. Then I would say sympathetically, "I totally get it. I once worked with a church in Southern California that wanted someone who didn't grow up in the church, had at least five years of experience, knew how to surf, and had a visible tattoo." (Completely true story, by the way.) As I told my story, I watched their faces subtly change, and I could read their minds. *Oh—that's what we're doing, isn't it?* They would realize they were getting a bit silly without knowing it. If I had told them so directly, they would have become defensive, but by telling the story of someone else, they realized I was telling their story too.

Fundamental #5: Create a Shared Experience

Coaching is about relationship, and nothing builds a relationship like a shared experience. Doing an activity together builds rapport, lowers barriers, and provides opportunities to discuss important matters in unexpected ways. One of the best ways to create a shared experience with your team is to **do something together that breaks new ground** for the person you are coaching and plants an unforgettable marker in your relationship with them.

A great example in Jesus's leadership life occurred when a crowd of five thousand men and their families were in a remote location with him and his disciples and had nothing to eat. Jesus assigned the disciples the task of feeding them all. They got flustered and protested that they could not afford anywhere near that much bread, so Jesus took the assignment to the next level by having them seat the crowd, collect a boy's five loaves and two fish, and distribute this meager lunch to the crowd of thousands. It made no sense at first, but as they did the work together and the food multiplied, they learned a lesson about Jesus they would never forget. It is no coincidence that this is the only miracle performed by Jesus that is recorded in all four Gospels.

My (Stan's) daughter Crystal struggled in college. She did not seem to even attempt to do well. My natural parental response was to urge her to get disciplined, buckle down, and do better. It was tempting to view the situation in terms of the "waste" of money already paid if Crystal did not get a degree. But the thing that bothered my wife, Connie, and me the most was that Crystal was unhappy and lacked direction. All in all, it was not a fun place for parents to be, much less for Crystal.

We had adopted Crystal, and we considered her to be God's gift to our family; this difficult season was not going to change that. So to get some relief, I thought back to the things that brought her joy, times that she was energized participating in something. All I had to do was walk into her room and see the paintings on her wall that she had painted either for art class or simply because she really loved to paint. Crystal always loved art, and I noticed that her passion for it was still strong even when her grades weren't.

Through an acquaintance, I learned of a school in Hollywood that trains elite makeup artists for work in film and in high-end salons and retail, and one summer day after her second year of college, I suggested to Crystal that we go check it out in person.

Crystal was wary; she had gotten so disheartened by school experiences that her hopes were not high, and she was sensitive to being pressured by her parents to make something work. But I played it as cool as possible, and Crystal grudgingly agreed.

When we walked into the building, it breathed a chic vibe that was unlike anything Crystal had ever encountered in a school before. She was captivated. I will never forget her grin that stretched from ear to ear as she looked around. She turned to me and said, "Dad, I love this place!" The people she saw there were doing exactly what she wanted to do.

That shared experience exploded the wall that blocked Crystal from her future and career, and I drove home with a more excited daughter than I had seen in a long time. As it turned out, Crystal attended and excelled in the school's intense, nine-month program, and today she is a highly skilled artist and team leader at Nordstrom's.

Obviously, our trip to the school in Hollywood was a win. But even if she had not gone to there—even if she had gone into some other artistic field—the experience would still have been a win because it broke Crystal out of her stuck pattern. (It broke

Figure 4: Going North

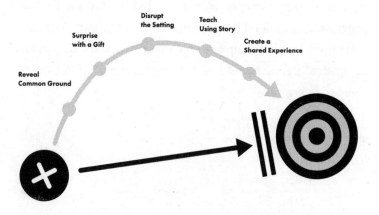

her parents out too.) That shared experience expanded Crystal's mind to new possibilities that were bound to move her forward.

A Change of Mind

Going North might seem like a savvy leadership technique, but it is actually deeply rooted in the practice of our faith and the key to much of the constructive change we experience in life.

Think for a moment about the spiritual disciplines: these are time-honored methods of Going North. We cannot make ourselves into better people; only the Holy Spirit can do that. But the spiritual disciplines are practices that exert indirect influence on our spiritual lives—they get around the barriers we erect that distance us from the Spirit's reconstructive work. Fasting, silence, prayer, even Bible reading do not change us per se; rather, they reposition our hearts and minds so the Spirit can better change us.

In the end, change is what we and the people we lead need most of all. And that too is at the core of our faith. The biblical word in English is *repentance*; its Greek counterpart is *metanoia*, meaning "a change of mind." That is what Going North provides. It is leadership that slides around the narrow blinders and limitations that trap a person in order to show them a more expansive view of themselves, their world, and all that God calls them to in their work.

CHAPTER 8

The New Normal

Acquiring the Habits That Help
People Love Their Work

IMPROVleadership is the art of helping people love their work so that their productivity goes up and turnover goes down. It makes your organization an attractive place to work, and it helps you keep your best people. It causes job opportunities coming from other organizations to ricochet off their hearts, and it inspires them to work together, performing at the highest level.

But this ideal does not happen by accident or even by aspiration. It comes out of a leader's intentional commitment to see their people as people and to take them seriously. It comes from relentless practice at serving the people who serve you. But it is dangerously easy for a leader to credit themselves with putting the right principles into practice when they merely agree with the principles but don't actually practice them.

A classic American business case study bears this out. In

IMPROVleadership is the art of helping people love their work so that their productivity goes up and turnover goes down. ☕

1955 the Ford Motor Company designed a brand-new model, the Edsel, which has since gone down in history as the auto industry's greatest flop. Ford lost $250 million on its huge gamble; put another way, for every Edsel that Ford sold, the company lost about that much money on a car it made but did not sell.

Many pundits of the era blamed the Edsel's failure on Ford's unprecedented, extensive market research. The company promised to deliver a car that accommodated the wishes of every American consumer, especially the young middle class. But the pundits were wrong—Ford's problem was not its focus groups and polling. Its problems came from what it did with the data it received.

In many cases, Ford simply ignored what people wanted. For example, advertising pros spent innumerable man-hours inventing and testing ideal names for the car, only for the chairman of the board to decide to throw out the research and name it after Henry Ford's son. And public input had no impact on the car's design at all.

At the other extreme, to the extent that Ford did take its research seriously, the result was to make a product that was supposed to be everything to everyone and therefore ended up being nothing to anyone. The eighteen variations on the basic concept did not appeal to buyers; rather, all those choices confused them. The Edsel was the remarkable combination of something both too generic and also too complicated to be any good.[1]

It is easy to laugh at Ford's blunders, but those types of mistakes may be more familiar than leaders care to admit. Supervisors face the same dangers in how they relate to their teams. Employees continually share information about themselves with anyone paying attention, but too often leaders ignore it. Instead, they default to treating everyone generically—as if they are all switched on by the same things—and their leadership suffers for it.

The bigger principle is that doing research on the people on your team and knowing what makes them tick won't matter if you don't implement what you learn. IMPROVleadership yields its amazing results only through **a process of hard work, repetition, and self-correction.** The great news is that you can do this. You do not have to be a natural "people person." You *do* have to devote time to IMPROVleadership as a priority in your day.

How to Grow as an IMPROVleader

We know we are not the first people to argue for the importance of "emotional intelligence."[2] We know there are assessment instruments to measure a leader's "EQ." These pile onto the same stack of self-diagnostic tools as Myers-Briggs, the Enneagram, CliftonStrengths, and so on.

We find value in such tools because they help people become more self-aware and more considerate of others on their team. But they also set a trap: once a person gets a label, they can misuse it to excuse themselves from improving in critical areas of their lives: "Hey, I can't help it—my top strength is Competition. . . . I'm an eight. . . . I don't have much Earth Green energy." They can also use it to pigeonhole others: "Yeah, you would think that way as an ISFJ. . . . You talk to her for me since you're an S."

Both of us resist any use of a tool that turns people into objects to work around and eliminates the possibility of growth. It's a cop-out from accountability, and it lacks courage and hope.

It also lacks faith that God is capable of changing a person to complete them in Christ.

Without disparaging legitimate uses of other systems, we submit that IMPROVleadership is different. Its five competencies contain tools to help you build better relationships and meet the emotional needs that all of us have. They are not inborn talents of the chosen few; **they are skills everyone can acquire.** It doesn't matter what your ability was when you picked up this book—you can improve!

When we share IMPROVleadership with others, many of them appreciate it because it resonates with what they naturally do. Ironically, senior leaders, who need it the most, appreciate it because it does *not* come naturally, yet they recognize their need for it. They want to become consciously competent in these skills. We encourage them that they can get there by taking new actions. They can heal the ongoing discomfort of their work situation through the temporary discomfort of learning a new way to live.

My wife and I (David) practically had our house rebuilt. All the interior walls were removed, and only the exterior walls were left standing. The builders had to put up poles and scaffolding to keep the roof from collapsing while they worked. But once they put new beams in, they could remove the artificial, temporary architecture they had installed, and the building could bear its weight again as a new house.

In the same way, acquiring the competencies of IMPROVleadership requires you to build a scaffolding around your work life, knock down old ways of leading, and build up new ones. **You construct artificial habits that do not come naturally until they become your new nature.**

Stan is a natural question-asker; I (David) am not. But I became one with practice. I didn't naturally show interest in team members' family lives until I punched reminders into my phone to ask about their kids' basketball games and performances in Christmas plays. I still use those calendaring disciplines today but not as often as before because the disciplines have changed me. Now I often ask questions and remember family activities by instinct. You too can build such habits into your life, and on the other side, you will be a better leader than you ever were before.

New Habits

There are all kinds of habits you can build into your life to allow the competencies of IMPROVleadership to take root. There are no limits to the options.

For instance, write "1-2-3" on the whiteboard in your office. **Commit to asking three significant questions each day**, whether for Story Mining, Lobbing Forward, or Going North. Look at your schedule, and strategize good times and places to do it. Every time you ask a significant question, cross off a number. The next day, rewrite the numbers and do it again.

Mix up your meetings—make them spaces to connect on a personal level with your team. Schedule an hour for a forty-five-minute meeting to allow for Story Mining. Meet in a different room so that people enter with an expectation that something different is going to happen.

After the meeting—or any other time—**write notes and reminders to ensure you caught the details of people's lives** to recall later, when you need them. Write a note on your phone

Acquiring the ☕ competencies of IMPROVleadership requires you to build a scaffolding around your work life, knock down old ways of leading, and build up new ones.

with the names of your team members' spouses and children. Put their spouses' birthdays on your calendar and send them a card from the organization. When their child has a major event, ask about it, text your team member while it is happening to tell them you are thinking about them, or maybe even attend it yourself. When a team member loses a loved one, set a reminder for the following year, and buy flowers to express sympathy that day. These gestures show people that you care for them as people; it doesn't matter to them what mechanism you use to "remember" the key details of their lives.

Breaking Out of Solitary

Another important step to take when learning IMPROVleadership is to **give someone on your team permission to call you on your "stuff."** All of us have the remarkable ability to see 360 degrees of other people's bodies but only 180 degrees of our own. Similarly, it is wise to assume that the people around you are better experts on your leadership than you are.

Understandably, some topics are so sensitive that either no team member wants to bring them up or you don't want to discuss them in house. This is one reason leaders **form a relationship with a coach.** Another benefit is that you can't go north on yourself when you are putting up resistance—only a coach can do that. Besides, how easily can you learn to coach your team if you have never been coached by someone else?

Dr. Atul Gawande is a surgeon at Brigham and Women's Hospital in Boston. After eight years he admitted to himself that his performance in the operating room had plateaued and was no longer improving. So Dr. Gawande invited a former professor of his to observe his surgery and coach him. Gawande says, "No matter how well-trained people are, few can sustain their best performance on their own." Outside eyes can see what no one else can.[3]

For example, when we coach senior pastors in large churches, time and again we see a plain-as-the-nose-on-your-face reality that is invisible to them: **the physical layout of their building is designed to frustrate their leadership.** The lead pastor has the office farthest away from common spaces. There is a door that they alone use to enter the building in the morning with a parking space reserved for them right next to it. Their executive assistant is located outside their office as a gatekeeper.

As a result, they are utterly insulated from the rest of the staff, and they have no reason to fraternize with them. Some staff never see the senior pastor except at a monthly all-staff meeting, and some senior pastors don't even make that if they are not leading it. When the senior pastor does walk into a part of the building they don't usually frequent, staff there tense up, anticipating either that they did something wrong or that a new assignment is on its way.

Lead pastors have a variety of ways to justify their isolation, claiming, for example, that it preserves their focus and maximizes their efforts, but they fail to calculate the toll it takes on their ability to lead. Relationally disconnected leadership is simply not effective. Knowing and caring about your people is not a task that can be delegated to a middle manager.

We have counseled lead pastors who are stuck in this sort of building setup to schedule three fifteen-minute breaks each day, varying the times, to **walk the floor for no other purpose than to interact with people.** Use a different bathroom for a change. Get coffee from a different coffee maker. Run into people by accident, on purpose. Have scripted, unscripted meetups.

Repetition

Repetition is critical to establishing a new skill and acquiring the confidence inherent in it that can produce a new way of life. **Repetition has remarkable power to change you even when you don't like what you are practicing.** It can even change your heart toward the people with whom you have a difficult time working and put relationships back together.

A church once called me (Stan) to mediate between two staff members in one of its ministries. The beloved leader of the ministry had recently been relieved of his position, and the rest of the ministry was grieving the loss. The new leader hired as a replacement (we'll call him Steve) clumsily stepped into the breach and claimed that God had put him in that role for that very season. His timing was terrible, and he offended some of the staff, who at that moment needed empathy more than anything else.

The focal point of conflict was between Steve and "Trent," a staff member who was especially close to the leader who had left. There was a vague hope that the tension would go away with time, but unresolved, it only got worse.

Eventually, I was called in to mediate between them and seek reconciliation. I got the two men together for a lunch . . . and another and another. The situation intensified to the point that Steve was ready to fire Trent for not being a "team player."

After about six lunches in six weeks, I told them, "I realize neither of you is in a good place with this. You're close to parting ways, and even attempting to resolve this situation has been a difficult process." *(Long pause.)* "So I'm asking both of you to agree to what I'm about to ask." *(Another long pause.)* "This is only a verbal contract, but here's what I'm asking: For thirty

Repetition has remarkable power to change you even when you don't like what you are practicing.

days, will you be kind and helpful to each other? Kind and helpful. That's all I'm asking. There are no expectations beyond this. You guys are working in the same ministry, and you'll have to communicate daily as you work on projects together. Whether you realize it or not, other staff members are watching how you interact. Your actions are hurting the entire team." They were startled and maybe a little ashamed at my request, but they agreed.

Things did not improve overnight, but enough hope was built over the thirty-day period that it led to another. Eventually Steve and Trent gained some positive traction in their relationship. They began to collaborate. They had healthy, productive conversations that gave them new momentum. They began to build a good working relationship, and today they are friends in a very successful ministry.

The key was that they had a specific instruction—"Be kind"—that they followed daily, even when they did not feel like it. Every time they had a resentful thought, every time they entered a tricky meeting, every time they had a chance to gossip, they remembered to be kind. They did not become kind to each other merely because they wanted to. They became kind because they practiced kindness—they worked their kindness muscle, and it grew stronger. As a result, they became stronger leaders.

Your Team Next Year

We are convinced that when a leader masters the skills of IMPROVleadership and practices them faithfully, the leader changes and so does the whole organization. We have provided numerous examples in this book of how that can work, but there are two more stories we want to tell.

One of our clients is an executive pastor who recently became the lead pastor of his church after his predecessor's retirement. It was a big challenge: people needed time to grieve the loss of a beloved leader as well as time to renew their optimism about the church's future. Additionally, the new pastor was formerly known by the church staff as a gatekeeper but now needed to be known as a vision caster. Meanwhile, the church was about to add a new campus for the first time.

Our client learned IMPROVleadership competencies from us and skillfully applied them in his leadership setting. He created a unified staff culture by Story Mining with his team and encouraging them to do the same. He started Lobbing Forward with the church to help them imagine where God might be taking them. The transition is going great.

Our own organization, Slingshot Group, recently underwent a major transition that moved people into new roles and even altered the commission structure under which much of our staff had been compensated. When you mess with people's money and disrupt their financial expectations, they tend to get touchy. But out of fifty-five members of our team, we lost only one. This is a testament to the work we have done over the years to practice what we preach about IMPROVleadership. It permeates our organization and makes it a place that people do not want to leave.

If IMPROVleadership gets organizations through intense times of transition like these, it can get them through anything. And transition is what organizational leadership is all about; the truth is that you are always transitioning from one thing to another; if you're not, your organization is dying. Organizations fail to move forward because their leaders have not been willing to learn what you have begun learning by reading this book.

We say "begun learning" because reading about it is just the beginning. **When you finish the last page, we encourage you to take inventory of how you're currently doing in these five competencies.** Give yourself a grade; establish a baseline. We also hope your curiosity about your people has been ignited as never before and that you will take a fresh first step toward your team.

My IMPROVIeadership Grades Today

COMPETENCY	GRADE
Story Mining	
Precision Praising	
Metaphor Cementing	
Lobbing Forward	
Going North	

Over the next ninety days, practice the competencies with repetition, and make changes in your pattern of leading. You will find yourself asking more and better questions, praising your people often, telling stories to draw people in and skirt their defenses, and inspiring them with metaphor-rich visions of their future.

One year from now, we hope you will open up this book again and look at the grades you gave yourself today. We hope you see how far you have come. We also hope that as you look at your team, you see them more engaged than ever and more productive than you knew was possible. We hope you see people continuing to work in an environment that they could not imagine leaving. We hope that, like a great improvising musician, you are more able than ever to draw on your talent, your training, and your experience to contribute just the right notes with just the right feeling at just the right moment.

As a leader, you face challenges. You have goals, pressures, and deadlines. You have urgent needs and important priorities that require the best of your team. Within your team you encounter challenges ranging from underperformance to lack of commitment, from failure to communicate to rivalry between teammates. These challenges require all your skills as a leader; you can only overcome them with a whole array of well-developed competencies. IMPROVleadership is about adding an entire suite of coaching skills to solve problems and accelerate excellence in your team in ways you never could before.

Every leader has projects on their plate. **We invite you to make IMPROVleadership project number one.** You won't regret it!

Notes

Chapter 1: The Cure for the Common Leader

1. Kent Shaffer, "Patrick Lencioni on Organizational Health," Preach It Teach It, https://www.preachitteachit.org/articles/detail/patrick-lencioni-on-organizational-health.

Chapter 2: All Part of the Job

1. Malcolm Gladwell, *Outliers: The Story of Success* (New York: Little, Brown and Company, 2008), chap. 2, NOOK.

Chapter 3: Story Mining

1. Marshall Goldsmith, "Have the Courage to Ask," May 2, 2005, https://www.marshallgoldsmith.com/articles/have-the-courage-to-ask.
2. Martin B. Copenhaver, *Jesus Is the Question: The 307 Questions Jesus Asked and the Three He Answered* (Nashville: Abingdon, 2014).
3. Chip Conley, *Wisdom at Work: The Making of a Modern Elder* (New York: Currency, 2018), 98.

Chapter 4: Precision Praising

1. C. S. Lewis, *Reflections on the Psalms* (New York: Harcourt, Brace & World, 1958), 93.
2. Lewis, *Reflections on the Psalms*, 95.
3. Scott Berinato, "Negative Feedback Rarely Leads to

Improvement," *Harvard Business Review* (January–
February 2018): 32–33, https://hbr.org/2018/01/negative
-feedback-rarely-leads-to-improvement.

4. Sally Jenkins, interview by John Yang, *PBS NewsHour*,
February 4, 2019, https://www.pbs.org/newshour/show/
the-details-and-discipline-behind-the-new-england-patriots
-unprecedented-success.

Chapter 5: Metaphor Cementing

1. Michael Chorost, "Your Brain on Metaphors," *Chronicle of Higher
Education*, September 21, 2014, https://www.chronicle.com/
article/Your-Brain-on-Metaphors/148495.

2. Leonard Sweet, *SoulTsunami: Sink or Swim in New Millennium
Culture* (Grand Rapids: Zondervan, 1999), 201.

3. Specifically, Jesus declined to use Greek leadership terms with
the prefix *arch-*, which carry strong authoritarian overtones.
When Jesus did use an *arch-* term, it was to tell his disciples
what *not* to do. For example, "You know that the rulers
[*archontes*] of the Gentiles lord it over them, and their high
officials exercise authority over them. Not so with you. Instead,
whoever wants to become great among you must be your
servant" (Matthew 20:25–26).

4. David W. Bennett, *Metaphors of Ministry: Biblical Images for
Leaders and Followers* (Eugene, OR: Wipf & Stock, 1993), 70–71.

5. Martin Luther King Jr., "'I Have a Dream,' Address Delivered
at the March on Washington for Jobs and Freedom," August
28, 1963, The Martin Luther King, Jr. Research and Education
Institute, Stanford University, https://kinginstitute.stanford.
edu/king-papers/documents/i-have-dream-address-delivered
-march-washington-jobs-and-freedom.

6. Marcus "Goodie" Goodloe, conversation with David A. Miller.

7. This phrase is how C. S. Lewis described why he wrote
imaginative fiction like the Chronicles of Narnia to
communicate the gospel. C. S. Lewis, *On Stories and Other*

Essays in Literature, ed. Walter Hooper (New York: Harvest, 1982), 47.

8. John Adair, *The Leadership of Jesus and Its Legacy Today* (Cleveland: Pilgrim, 2002), 125–26.

Chapter 6: Lobbing Forward

1. Oliver Wendell Holmes, *The Autocrat of the Breakfast-Table* (Boston: Osgood & Co., 1873), chap. 9, http://www.gutenberg .org/files/751/751-h/751-h.htm.

2. Will Mancini, *Church Unique: How Missional Leaders Cast Vision, Capture Culture, and Create Movement* (San Francisco: Jossey-Bass, 2008), 80.

Chapter 8: The New Normal

1. Richard Feloni, "4 Lessons from the Failure of the Ford Edsel, One of Bill Gates' Favorite Case Studies," *Business Insider*, September 5, 2015, https://www.businessinsider.com/ lessons-from-the-failure-of-the-ford-edsel-2015-9.

2. See, for example, Daniel Goleman, Richard Boyatzis, and Annie McKee, *Primal Leadership: Unleashing the Power of Emotional Intelligence* (Boston: Harvard Business Review Press, 2013).

3. Atul Gawande, "Personal Best," The New Yorker, September 26, 2011, https://www.newyorker.com/magazine/2011/10/03/ personal-best.

Slingshot Group builds remarkable teams through staffing and coaching.

At Slingshot Group, our people and our process set us apart. Every one of our associates has ministry experience and knows what it takes to hire great staff. We're growing the kingdom by helping put the right people in the right place and coaching them to reach their fullest potential. In fact, Slingshot guarantees the placement of staff with no time constraints on search. We'll even coach your team along the way—because that's what partners do.

Get Started: slingshotgroup.org/staffing

IMPROVleadership™

A course created by experienced pastors and church leaders.

DESIGNED FOR THE REAL WORLD.

IMPROVleadership™ online coaching is a first-of-its-kind training that brings Slingshot Group's unique coaching techniques directly to your phone or laptop, where you can learn on your own time. Take what you learned in the book one step further with access to **training videos, leadership tools, and Slingshot coaches** who will provide insight and challenge how you lead in your church or ministry.

Sign up today to get:

- Thirty-eight videos covering the five competencies of IMPROVleadership
- Work-at-your-own-pace lessons designed for those in full-time ministry. Complete the course in only five days or take five weeks—it's up to you.
- Tools that help you get more out of your leadership and your team
- Exclusive access to Slingshot coaches via the Slack app

Become a better leader in just five days.

Sign Up: slingshotgroup.org/improv

LAUNCH
THE FIRST 90 DAYS

Take your new hires to the next level.

When a new hire begins working at your ministry or organization, the first ninety days are a critical time for them to get onboarded and start well. Studies show that how you navigate this window of time will determine how quickly new staff members bring value to their new roles in the short term and add value to your team and organization in the long term.

As leaders, how can we ensure new hires are set up for success starting on day one? In Slingshot Group's white paper *Top 5 Mistakes New Hires Make in Their First 90 Days (And How Coaching Can Help Them Avoid These Pitfalls)*, you'll learn about the benefits of investing in new hires from the onset—so you can avoid the most common mistakes people make when they start a new role.

Download Now: slingshotgroup.org/resources